27.03.2

To Michael -
    Congratulations on
I hope you enjoy reading this book -
bringing back memories of your youth in
                                    Omagh

Sean Sheridan was born in Omagh, a small country town in Northern Ireland, and
was educated locally by the Christian Brothers. He lived in London from the age of
19 and worked initially in the fund management industry and later in global banking
with RBS and HSBC. He is a fellow of the Chartered Institute of Securities and
Investments but his first job upon arriving in London was that of a stripper's assistant
in a North London pub, a role that never appeared on his CV.

Best wishes
    From your Cousins -
        Joan & Kevin

For Cassie Ann, a woman of indomitable spirit.

Sean Sheridan

A Mother's Tale

AUSTIN MACAULEY PUBLISHERS™

LONDON * CAMBRIDGE * NEW YORK * SHARJAH

All of the events in this memoir are true to the best of author's memory. The views expressed in this memoir are solely those of the author.

A CIP catalogue record for this title is available from the British Library.

ISBN 9781398404113 (Paperback)
ISBN 9781398404120 (ePub e-book)

www.austinmacauley.com

First Published 2022
Austin Macauley Publishers Ltd®
1 Canada Square
Canary Wharf
London
E14 5AA

A big thank you to the team at Austin Macauley for having faith in me to publish this book and for all their guidance, help and, most of all, their patience.

Grateful thanks to Mark McGrath for access to his wealth of photos and pictorial records.

Abbey Street

She caught me peeking at her from beneath my blanket as she squatted over the bucket in near darkness to have a pee.

"Go to sleep, Son," she whispered quietly. A mixture of embarrassment and annoyance in her voice. I closed my eyes and pretended to be asleep. But I could still hear the gushing sounds and detect the smell of her steaming pee as it hit the bottom of the empty aluminium bucket. The 'Pish Bucket', as it was known in our house.

"Sleep, child," she whispered again but more forcibly this time. I did, eventually.

Cassie Ann was born on a remote farm in rural Donegal. A couple of cows, a pig for the bacon that was slaughtered and cured in the house and a few hens for the fresh eggs were the entire contents of the smallholding. She was christened, Catherine Ann, but from an early age was always referred to as Cassie Ann, a name that she enjoyed for the rest of her life. Before Cassie Ann was born, her father had died in a drowning accident in the Atlantic Ocean off the coast of Bundoran. For the sake of survival, her mother remarried an aged neighbouring bachelor farmer who reluctantly adopted the young Cassie Ann. She never spoke of her life growing up on the farm and not a word was said about her stepfather even on that cold winter's night when a member of the Royal Ulster Constabulary knocked hard on our front door and announced that her stepfather had been discovered dead in his bed in far-off Donegal and required burying. She disappeared for a few days and when she returned, she never mentioned him ever again. We never even knew his name.

After their marriage, Cassie Ann and my father, Felix, scraped enough money together to buy a rambling wreck of a house on Abbey Street, in a small provincial town in Tyrone, not far inside the northern side of the heavily fortified British border. It was in the Abbey Street house that I was born under the watchful eyes of the local midwife, Nurse Meek. She was the maternity nurse who delivered all the new-born babies within the vicinity of Abbey Street, Castle Street and Brook Street. Nurse Meek, and her trusty Mary Jane bicycle, were a constant presence in the locality. She was a busy nurse having to tend to the needs of the ever-expanding Catholic families where the practice of contraception was forbidden by the clergy and greedily ignored by the menfolk. Her arrival on the street riding the oversized bicycle would be greeted with cheers from the youngsters and much whispering from the local women.

"That'll be another one for that poor McGuigan woman to add to the ten she already has. God Bless her," was the usual response from the neighbours.

Nurse Meek would take a large medical bag from the pannier on the front of her Mary Jane bicycle and hurry to one of the houses, and behind closed doors, she would deliver yet another wailing addition to the already overpopulated world.

Our house in Abbey Street was situated between a grocery shop at one end, the Brook Street end where the local unemployed layabouts would gather to annoy passers-by each afternoon and, at the other end of the street a workshop for storing coffins owned by the local undertaker, a garrulous and very friendly Charlie Doherty. It was a busy thoroughfare located at the bottom of Castle Street, so-called, allegedly, because a Norman castle once towered over the town from the site that was located there. Why the French thought it a clever idea to set off from Normandy and establish a castle in such a remote area of Ireland was never fully understood by the locals. Still, it was a handy name for a very steep street. Abbey Street was one of the main routes leading into the small, but very busy market town. God-fearing people would pass our front door on their way to their daily ritual of 10 o'clock Mass in the Sacred Heart Church, a grandiose edifice perched high up on the hill opposite the less pretentious and less frequently attended Protestant Church of Ireland building.

There were four churches of numerous religious denominations within 200 yards spitting distance from each other. And on certain days of the year, the Orange Marching season in July, in particular, those attending their respective services would forcibly eject the occasional phlegm from their religious mouths at each other. Sadly though, whilst the town was blessed with so many places of worship, we were short on Christianity and still are.

Sunday was a day of prayer across the North of Ireland, whether you were a heathen, agnostic or a Christian. Children's playgrounds were locked up, chains were hung across the slides and swings, the pubs and shops were closed, streets deserted and even the cinema was banned from opening. It was the Lord's Day and a day for reading the good book and the Holy Scriptures, not a day for sinful pleasures for God-fearing folk in the predominantly Protestant North of Ireland. Catholic churches would be packed from early morning with parishioners flocking to one of four Masses during the early sessions. Most Catholics attended Mass as families and the sight of a group of eight or ten taking up a whole pew was not unusual. The Catholic Church, like so many religious institutions, is a business. Show business in fact. It has profit and loss accounts and balance sheets, and Sundays were the days when money was to be had from the captive, but occasionally unwilling or impoverished Parishioners. Schools and the church building required maintenance and upkeep, the gardens and lawn had to be kept immaculate and the priests had to have the latest make of car with which to visit the housebound, the golf club and those on their death beds. The baskets would be circulated from the front and back rows of pews and would be passed from worshipper to worshipper with each looking at the amount dropped in the basket by the previous person. No change was permitted. Watching the baskets laden down with coins and notes being taken to the altar and placed there for the Celebrant Priest to look down upon, usually with a broad smile on his face, was sometimes a bit too much for Cassie Ann to accept.

"Hope it chokes them," she could be heard muttering under her voice but just loud enough for those nearby to hear her.

Death was a constant companion in Abbey Street. Seldom would a day pass without the news of another neighbour or distant relative falling off the perch, and the gossip in the streets was such that news of someone's demise was spread far and wide within hours of them taking their last breath. And occasionally before that last breath. Sometimes, death was a bit premature for some old perpetually dying old fogey. The women would gather outside each other's houses and discuss, in great detail, the reasons for the death and speculate as to how long she or he had been suffering from whatever ailment that finally took the unfortunate person to meet their maker.

"Good God Almighty but he did suffer, the poor auld bastard. But he is gone now and at peace. Mind you, his Missus doesn't look too miserable. There must be a tidy wee insurance policy tucked away somewhere. There'll be new frocks and shoes for that one just you mark my words."

"Where's the Wake being held, Mrs?" would be one of the first questions.

"He's a big family so they'll have to squeeze him into that wee bedroom at the front. He couldn't do the stairs, the poor crater. There'll be plenty going to it. Jesus, he was a lovely man. Pity he married that wan though. He was far too good-looking for the likes of her. Face like a battered fart and all skirt and no knickers."

The Catholic Church enjoyed a good funeral. Plenty of money to be had, especially if the deceased came from one of the few well-off families in the town, and there was a sprinkling of them: publicans, doctors and solicitors. Cassie Ann once took me to a Requiem Mass for a near neighbour when I was about six or seven years old. At a late stage of the proceedings, the celebrant ascended the high pulpit wearing his richly decorated symbolic black vestment that he wore for funerals. He began to read from a large book with a red cover which he held in his left hand and with the index finger of his right hand he pointed to each name on the list of people in the congregation who had contributed to the

Requiem Mass. This was known as the 'Offering' for the Mass. In practice, it was meant to be a form of almsgiving for those priests who lived in poverty and gave their time and energy looking after their impoverished congregations. In our case, it was the well-off priest taking money they could ill afford from the mostly poverty-stricken gathering at Funeral Masses.

"Doctor Mc Guigan, £20," the priest's voice loud, slow and strong.

"Mrs Campbell, £15," referring to the owner of the local pharmacy the voice just as strong.

"Mr John McLaughlin, £15," referring to the owner of a furniture store in the town, the voice becoming slightly lower in tone.

"Michael Nugent, £5," from the man who owned the local grocery shop, the priest's voice now dropping a few decibels.

"Mrs Noble, 10 shillings," a near neighbour with seven young children, his voice now taking on a much harsher tone.

"Mrs Cassie Ann McCaffrey, 2 shillings," his voice now sounding distinctly harsh and disparaging, almost contemptible. Cassie Ann just looked at the floor for the remainder of the Mass and mumbled some inaudible prayers, or at least I thought that they were prayers.

After a few more names were hurriedly announced, the elegantly attired man of God and Mammon closed the Book, turned towards the altar, descended the pulpit and went directly to centre stage in front of the tabernacle. He had concluded the reading of the day's offerings from the grateful, and some not so grateful, parishioners at the funeral of one of the well-to-do members of his congregation. Thankfully, the days of the offerings ended later in my childhood but the memory of the humiliation of an impoverished Cassie Ann by a well-fed cleric of the Catholic Church, lived with me long after she had passed away.

Sunday may have been a day of prayer and bible reading for everyone across the country, but the Catholics contrived to organise dances on the evening of the Lord's Day in Saint Joseph's Parish Hall. This was a building owned and strictly governed by the Catholic Church. As such, any event required the presence and the ever-watchful eyes of the local clergy to oversee the activities of the evening. Forever looking to fill the bottomless coffers of the church, the Parish Priest and his cohorts would charge admission to the hall and permit the sale of soft drinks only to the youthful audience. The sale of alcohol, more commonly known among teetotallers as the Devil's Brew, was strictly forbidden. It was the duty of the young curates of the Parish to ensure that couples maintained a discreet distance from each other when the slow dances were being played and woe betide any couple, or individual, who would attempt any serious touching or groping during their musical romp. It was as if a plague was about to descend upon the young dancers since the enforced requirement to stay distant from one's partner, so as to ensure there was little likelihood of passing on whatever disease might be doing the rounds at the time. The curate's eyes were everywhere; looking at who was getting just that bit closer than permitted or whose hands were reaching parts of the female anatomy that was positively out of bounds and strictly against the laws of God. At times though, the young curate could be seen glancing for just that few seconds too long in the direction of some well-endowed, good-looking girls who may have just caught his eye. It would be a confession in the morning for the curate, or possibly not.

Strong drink was never far away from these gatherings though. Local young men, deprived of how to act around young nubile girls, required a level of courage to engage with members of the fairer sex and that audacity only came after a few sips of strong drink. The workings of the mind and the bodies of females were alien to virgin lads but a couple of sups of vodka from a quarter bottle purchased in Broderick's on the Saturday before turned a young spotty lad into the Don Juan of the Derry Road, or the Casanova of Castle Street in no time at all. Cheap alcohol was always an effective way to lift the spirits before entering the fray in the Parish Hall, but the vigilante curates such as the cunning Father Clerkin, the curate of curates, could detect the smell of alcohol from a great distance. With a nose like a Pinocchio Lizard, it was so pointed that that it was said he could pick up a bun from the floor with it, Clerkin would patrol the dance floor like a man with a mission to protect the local youth from the sins of the flesh. His never-ending clerical objective in life was to ensure that young men and women kept a discreet distance from each other when dancing along to some slow cheesy waltz played on a wonky record by some heathen English group. None of that close hugging or whispering in ears or even jiving, a dance that the locals had a great preference for. Distance had to be maintained in case bodily fluids might have been stirred and possibly shaken. Crafty Clerkin was destined for much higher office in the Church, so he undertook his responsibilities, the protection of horny teenagers from themselves, with great gusto; and the mere sight of his virgin white clerical collar and his pointed nose on the periphery of the dance floor was more than enough of a deterrent for lads to keep as far away from their dancing partners as was physically possible.

But he was nowhere to be found when the dancing finished and the girls required escorting home. It was then that the real dancing and pocket billiards began.

The Drink (Sometimes Known as Alcohol)

Ireland has had a long and sometimes, despairing reputation for the love of alcohol and the men of the town, and some women, were no exception. Poverty and despair were in abundance and men, who had little money, would often squander whatever cash they could find on cheap drink at the expense of the well-being of their large families. A half-bottle of Red Biddy, a cheap fortified wine and the Buckfast of its day, would leave a man paralytic and raring for a fight with any passer-by whom he might take a dislike to. The inevitable outcome would be a visit from a couple of members of the Royal Ulster Constabulary and a few whacks on the back of the head with a regulation police baton followed by a restless night's sleep in the local police station.

Three public houses could be found within throwing-up distance from our house. O'Kane's and Gormley's, directly opposite each other on the street halfway up the steep Castle Street hill. At the bottom of Abbey Street nestled The Military Arms, named in honour of the nearby local British Army Barracks and its transient English inhabitants. To the locals it was known as Friel's' Pub after its owner, Jimmy Friel, a shrewd little man with horn-rimmed spectacles, but to Cassie Ann, it was 'that place of sin and wickedness' where men talked shite all evening and staggered home after closing time looking for a bite to eat and instead getting an earful from the long-suffering Mrs. The only women who would frequent such establishments were sinful and of bad character; she would announce to anyone within earshot.

'Hoors' as she would call them. She was not a great lover of alcohol, and of those who partook, and would loudly proclaim her disgust at any man she discovered intoxicated, including her husband and my long-suffering father who enjoyed the occasional bottle of Guinness or two.

If there was money to be had, Friel's was the place to have a few drinks. But on Friday evenings, on the way home from their work driving pig and cattle lorries from local farms to the abattoir, my father and his brothers would invariably end up in Gormley's, a very rough and ready shambolic public house that attracted the most engaging of the town's characters. The pub was run by its charming owner, Mickey Gormley and his two spinster sisters, Bridie and Annie, a pair of formidable women and more than enough for any man who had the temerity to annoy or cross the sisters. Traditional singers and fiddlers would frequently provide the regulars with a couple of songs and a merry jig or two in exchange for a few pints of Porter. Fights were common especially when payment for a round of drinks was not forthcoming resulting in a couple of black eyes and the occasional broken nose. But Mickey was a man who would stand for no nonsense from anyone, and once barred, the culprit would remain firmly excluded until apologies were forthcoming and the swelling on the eyes had subsided. And drinks all paid for.

In its day, Gormley's mirrored so many other drinking establishments across Ireland. Part drinking den, part community centre, part confessional, part dealing house, and most important of all, a hiding place from angry wives awaiting their dole money to buy food for the children. It was the practice for each pub to bottle their own Guinness and Porter. The beers would be sent from the brewery in wooden kegs and delivered to the pub cellar, where an apprentice, or the owner, made sure that it was carefully poured into a bottle. The keg was tapped but it was so heavy that it couldn't be lifted to any decent height. This meant that the unfortunate lad responsible for filling the bottles could only get it up a small bit and the person doing the pouring had to sit on a small stool, hunched over.

The pubs had to wash their own bottles once the content was consumed by the customer at the counter and ensure that they were clean and ready for a new brew. The bottles would be soaked to remove the labels, and also scrubbed on the inside with a bristled bottle-washing brush. Each pub would have their own label, with the name of the pub on it and with the label having to be stuck on the bottle using a paste of flour and water. There were no metal caps for bottles, so a cork would be inserted using a press specifically made for this function. Most public houses were privately owned and run by generations of families. However, it was a requirement to take on apprentices for up to four years after which they would be considered as qualified to be a fully competent barman.

Priests were seldom seen in pubs. Frequently, the priests with bulbous red noses would berate the audience as to the perils of alcohol and would urge their flock to avoid having anything to do with Satan's Mouthwash. However, the same priests would have the occasional tipple in the sanctuary of the Parochial House where all manner of alcohol would be delivered to them for their own consumption. The rare occasion when a priest would pop into a public house would be to check-up on those parishioners who would be seen proudly wearing a pin on their lapels to denote that they were teetotal and never took drink. Some lapsed though and the ever-nosey priests would be only too happy to scour the pubs of the town looking for such culprits. It was also the days before wine was distributed at Mass. Such a notion would never receive approval from the bishops especially in Ireland, the land of Saints and Drunkards. Nonetheless, the local priests thoroughly enjoyed sampling wines from their vast collection. As for Communion a thin wafer of blessed bread was more than enough for the communicants on a cold Sunday morning.

The toilet facilities in Gormley's were not of a standard that would be considered as welcoming. It was a man's drinking den and the basic facilities were provided without complaint from the consumers of alcohol. When a bladder was full, the customer would be required to stand at a wall out in the yard and pee into a gutter running along its length. Those wishing to use a toilet for the other business would be required to beg Mickey, or God Forbid, his sisters, for the use of their lavatory—not something that was overly welcomed by the family. The only female visitors to Gormley's were a couple of women from the travelling community. They were known as gypsies back then and wore heavy shawls over long skirts and strong boots. When they had their fill of bottles of Guinness, they would quietly sneak out to the backyard, hoist up their skirts and squat. A pish or a big shite was not a bother to them. Then back to the drinking and smoking in the bar.

Pubs were for drinking, chatting about slow horses and nagging wives and smoking, of course. It was almost compulsory for the customers in the pub to smoke with the preference being Players untipped or Woodbine, both of which could be purchased in the bar and smoked there to their customers hearts' and lungs' content. At times, some intoxicated smokers might have two cigarettes on the go with one in the ashtray and one tucked between the heavily nicotine-stained fingers. Smoking accompanied drinking in the same way as butter went with bread, except with the latter there was less likelihood of dying early from lung cancer. Televisions were seldom permitted in pubs. In most cases those that possessed a television in their houses, and there were very few of them, it was invariably black and white as colour had yet to be invented and the number of available channels was limited. Television was not to be an infernal distraction from gossip and drinking in Gormley's pub in Castle Street for many years to come.

Saturday afternoons in the local public houses were the highlight of the week in the town. Drinking in pubs and gambling on horses went hand-in-hand, with many Irishmen believing that horseracing was in their blood and their DNA. There was a self-belief from Irishmen who claim they knew the merits of a horse and its ability to win a race that they would place bets on it even if they couldn't afford it. If there was even the remotest chance that a local horse would win a big race in Leopardstown or Fairyhouse, or even Down Royal, punters would beg, steal or borrow to ensure that they were on the winner. Sadly, for these eternally optimistic punters, the only winners were the bookies, of which there were several well-fed owners of such premises in the town. For some dastardly reason, many betting shops were located near the pubs or perhaps it was the other way around. Suffice to say that the form of the horses could be studied in the racing pages of the Irish News or the Daily Mirror and a bet hurriedly scribbled out and placed with the bookie on the other side of the street before the ink was dry.

One punter, who used to play the drums in a showband but now spent his afternoons and evenings in the pub, was inaptly named Lucky McCrumlish. His real name, and indeed his stage name, was John, but he acquired the sobriquet,

Lucky, due to his innate ability to select a nailed-on sure-fire loser, which when known to his punting pals, they would bet on some other nag in the same race to beat Lucky's animal. Lucky's selection always seemed to be nearer the back of the field rather than the front.

"My day will come. Just you wait and see you cheeky brats," he would hiss at them through his toothless gums. Lucky, although not the greatest tipster that had ever been born, was one of most loved characters in the town.

Most Friday evenings Cassie Ann would instruct me to run up to Gormley's Pub to extricate my father from his carousing with his brothers and his friends. Friday evening after work was the only time that he was permitted to have a few bottles of the brown stuff and he certainly made the most of it. Cassie Ann did not approve of these drinking sessions, especially as Confessions would be in full flow in the church a few hundred yards up the hill and decent people passing by would witness such behaviour and not be amused by such goings on. But she made a concession for a few hours every Friday after he picked up his wage packet from his employers at the Ulster Transport Authority for delivering pigs to the abattoir. Cassie Ann's recurring weekly plan was for me to entice him home before he spent the entire contents of the much-needed weekly wages on strong drinks and cheap fags. He was never so foolish, or brave, to spend it all, but Cassie Ann would always have a contingency plan, just in case. Felix, my uncles, Francie and Jim, and his pals from work would be enjoying an evening's drinking and boisterousness so much so that a request from a youngster tugging at the end of his jacket and begging him to return home, was invariably lost in the smoke, noise and alcohol fumes of the pub. The plan seldom worked. Invariably, I, and several other children of a similar age, would be left sitting outside the pub drinking from a bottle of red lemonade and eating Tayto crisps bought by the tipsy fathers to appease us young ones. He would eventually appear, somewhat well lubricated but always in a great mood and, as always, singing *The Hills above Drumquin* in memory of the village where he was born. Arriving at the front door, slightly the worse for wear, Felix always received the same welcome.

"Out drinking all night and spending your hard-earned money with the likes of those good for nothings," was Cassie Ann's weekly response. It seldom differed except for the occasional:

"Would you just look at the state of him, for heaven's sake. He would shame a body," she would sometimes shout especially if he was a wee bit too tipsy.

The next morning, all would be well again. For a little while.

There were lots of angry teetotal mothers in our street every Friday evening. And quite a few happy fathers, for a few hours at least.

There were four youngsters in our family, three boys and a sister Maureen who was the eldest. She was baptised Mary but my mother insisted on calling her Maureen 'for short' as she informed me many years later. I didn't dare argue with Cassie Ann as to the merits of Maureen being short for Mary. It was a strict requirement of the Catholic Church that all new-born children are named in honour of a saint, which is why we have so many Patricks and Marys in the country. Should any parent be so brave as to attempt to have a child baptised in any other name than that of the saints, the priest would exercise his divine right to overrule them and on occasions name the child as he saw fit. An Elvis McCaffrey most certainly would not have been tolerated by the all-knowing, always in charge, Catholic clerics.

Cassie Ann had given birth to another three young ones before I made my appearance into that troubled world. All of them had died shortly after birth. I never knew their names, nor was there ever any mention of them. It's as if they never existed. All new-born unbaptised infants were buried in separate, unmarked graves outside the walls of Killyclogher Cemetery. The rule of the Church then was that babies had to be baptised in the Catholic faith, otherwise it was a quick burial in an anonymous deep hole in un-consecrated ground away from the blessed souls of the baptised Catholics. These three innocents did not live long enough to receive the Sacrament of Baptism by a God-loving priest, and consequently, they were deemed to have been born with Original Sin on their souls. Damned at birth and not even an opportunity to commit a few sins. There was certainly nothing original about their unceremonious disposal though. A lost hole in the ground, no headstone to acknowledge their very existence and simply forgotten as an unfortunate afterthought. Except for the grieving parents, of course. The mother would grieve and be told that another little one would arrive in 9 months-time that would eradicate the memory of that impure baby who died with Original Sin on its soul. It was God's will, of course.

There was a constant air of happiness in that Abbey Street house. Cassie Ann was from Donegal in the Irish Republic, a few miles from the British border, and had her own usage of combined Irish and English languages. It's as if she had a command of neither but a wonderful knack of using both languages in a single sentence, much to the amusement of our innocent young ears. The older sister

20

would receive an ear bashing for being late home from the *damhsa* which was the Irish word for 'dance' and Cassie Ann would often say her prayers in her native Irish language interspersed with the occasional words of English that confused us no end. Occasionally, we would catch sight of Felix when she was in full flow using both languages, and smile at him as his bushy eyebrows would be raised to the high heavens in bewilderment. We assumed all families spoke in this manner and it was only as we grew older that it was apparent that Cassie Ann was multilingual in her own peculiar manner. Neighbours would call in to *ceili* for a while, or for a *comhairle*, Irish expressions that the locals would use for visiting each other on an evening. They would while away the early evening hours drinking cups of tea, eating fresh homemade soda bread and catching up on the local gossip, who had recently died, when was the next Wake and what time was the funeral. Death and dying were constant topics during these visits. Wakes were always of great interest in the local community.

Lodgers

To earn some much-needed extra money, Cassie Ann would take in lodgers and put them up in one of the few spare rooms we had in the old house. Sometimes they would stay a few nights, some might stay for months depending upon what their jobs were in the locality and some, like Uncle Johnny, would stay forever. Lodgers were a major source of additional income, but on occasions, they were inclined to spend their weekly wages on backing slow horses and consuming too much alcohol, usually on Friday evenings after work. Cassie Ann had little bother manhandling a few drunks after late-night sessions. It was her house and she was always the boss. Nobody was brave enough to argue with her when she was in full flow with a poker in her right hand.

Jack Groogan was a dapper man of uncertain years. How he came to be living with us was a mystery, since he seemed to have a much higher level of intelligence and assuredness than other lodgers who passed through our house. And he didn't appear to work for a living. Jack had a well-groomed moustache which he cultivated and groomed into a shape that resembled a British star of the screen that we would only see in some mystery film in the County Cinema on a Saturday morning. There was a military bearing about Jack who would regale us with tall tales of distant places and hot climates that we could only dream about.

Great Aunt Bridget, or Biddy, as she was known to the family and neighbours, was 83 and lived with us until she passed away when I was 7-years-

21

old. She never wore her false teeth and her gums could chew hard tobacco that she claimed eased the pains in her joints. Biddy, a frail but argumentative little lady, wore a long black shawl around her head and neck and was constantly checking her nose for anything chewable. Her hobby was knitting. She wasn't very good at knitting but she persisted and we were her models for whatever garment she contrived to manufacture with her needles.

Balaclavas were Biddy's speciality. Long before the local paramilitaries were disguising their faces, Cassie Ann's boys were required to wear Biddy's all-weather head, face and ear warmers. Problem was that Biddy had difficulties with proportionality. The black and partly blue headwear that I was provided with by the short-sighted great aunt had the eye sockets too far apart for a mere youngster. The mouth was at such an obtuse angle that the only way that I was able to navigate the footpath was to angle the balaclava so that one eye could see with the other one blind. To add to the confusion the slit for the mouth was closer to the left ear than my orifice. The winter months were bitterly cold so we were forced to adorn ourselves with these pre-IRA prototype ill-fitting headgear. And we looked totally ridiculous walking back and forth to school. Mainly sideways to be exact.

When Biddy eventually hung up her knitting needles the balaclavas were consigned to a bottom drawer in the back bedroom and gratefully forgotten. Never did I believe that balaclavas would catch on with our friends in the various terrorist organisations but I suppose someone else's aunt could knit properly.

Kirk from Dunkirk

We loved quiet, wee pipe-smoking Johnny Kirk. He wore a heavily sweat-stained flat cap at a quirky angle which covered the bald patches on his head. His one pleasure in life was his pipe which he used to fill with rubbed tobacco which he carved from a little block with his penknife. The ritual of carving the tobacco, rubbing it between the palms of his hands and then gradually filling the pipe was both intricate and time-consuming, but our Johnny was a master pipe smoker and clearly loved his art. He would pack the bowl of his pipe with the shards of tobacco, flatten it with his box of Swan Vesta matches, take a couple of hard pulls to help light the contents and watch as alarming spouts of flame would erupt. And that was before his first inhale of the actual tobacco. Johnny also enjoyed the occasional bottle of Guinness and a glass of Powers Whiskey or two after he picked up his weekly pension from the Post Office. But never to excess.

Cassie Ann did not approve and Johnny was respectful of her wishes. He was also probably reluctant to upset her as well.

"You know, Son, there are bad people in this world and you should do your best to avoid them," said Johnny looking down at me from the rickety old rocking chair.

"My mammy says bad people all go to hell when they die," I replied.

"I'm not too sure where hell is wee man but if I ever get close, I will send you a message to let you know."

"Ach, Johnny, you won't be going anywhere near hell. My mammy says you are a good man,"

"Awe now, Son, I have had my times both good and bad. Put some more turf on the fire. That's a good boy."

"What did you do in that war, Uncle Johnny?" I asked.

"Not a whole lot, Son, if I'm honest," he sighed and slowly leant forward so he could look directly into my eyes as I knelt at his feet.

"War is a terrible thing and brings out the worst in people, even good people. There was a day a long time ago when we were caught in crossfire on a wee road near a place called Dunkirk in France and the shooting was fierce. But we were the lucky ones because the driver of the lorry sped away towards the beach where we found hundreds of other soldiers hiding in the sand dunes." said Johnny.

"You must have been really scared though?"

"Aye, that I was, Son, but there was no time for fear as the guns kept firing from all directions and we buried ourselves in the sand as best we could. After a few days, our officers told us we were to surrender, and that we would be treated well by the Germans. They always lied, Son. We suffered many years of brutality, and for what? Anyway, that was the end of the war for me right there in the sand dunes of Dunkirk and not a bullet did I ever fire. Kirk from Dunkirk they would call me for many a year afterwards," he whispered, barely audible, "Kirk from Dunkirk my arse indeed."

Johnny stared at the ground for a long time, took a slow pull on his pipe, blew out the smoke and sat back in his chair looking deep into the flames. There was a look of sadness and melancholy about Johnny as the shadows of the flames danced across his tired and wrinkled face.

After his release from a German Prisoner of War camp in 1945, he returned to Ireland to discover that his young wife had divorced him and had taken up with an American soldier who was stationed in Derry. She disappeared to the

States, never to be seen or heard from again. Johnny was left not only loveless but also homeless. American soldiers had been stationed all over the North of Ireland in preparation for the D Day landings and their dashing uniforms and abundance of nylon stockings and cigarettes, and money of course, made them an instant hit with the impoverished local girls, both single and married. It was one of these temporary invaders that Johnny's wife fell for and eventually eloped to Idaho with him. Not even a letter to say goodbye and never was she heard from ever after.

And so, Johnny became our lodger and an integral part of the family. He found a job with the Post Office and spent the remaining years of his working life sorting and delivering letters and parcels around the countryside. Johnny remained our lodger until he passed away peacefully in his sleep with his cap on his bald head to keep it warm.

I was 14 when Johnny died at the ripe old age of 82 years. Mammy had sent me up to his bedroom one morning with a cup of strong tea to help Johnny welcome the day and there was our Johnny, ashen-faced and still. He had found peace finally. When Doctor McMullan confirmed his death from natural causes, Felix arranged for Johnny to be waked in our front room, the room that was only used when the Parish Priest or my Mammy's aunt, Sister Martha, from the Loreto Convent visited. A Wake is a celebration of the life of the deceased and not only did we pray and cry over our Johnny, but there was also much drinking and singing as Johnny would most certainly have approved.

After the wake and Johnny's subsequent funeral and internment in Killyclogher graveyard, we returned home. My Mammy and Daddy cleared away all Johnny's possessions and gave the good clothes to the local St. Vincent de Paul charity. The rest of his garments were consigned to the bin.

Many years later, I returned to my home on a visit from London following the deaths of my parents. I dawdled in each empty room soaking up the many memories now represented by bare walls and the threadbare carpet on every floor except the kitchen. I eventually found myself in what was Johnny's old bedroom and stood looking down at the stained mattress where he had slept for so many years. No one had occupied that room since Johnny's passing and the air was heavy and still with a musty, nicotine smell. I opened the thin curtains and all was just as it was when Johnny was removed from that tiny bedroom. Even the little moth-eaten chest of drawers by his bed containing his war medals was still there.

And there was his pipe. It was neatly packed with Gallagher's plug tobacco ready to be lit and smoked.

I stared at the pipe for ages and thought of those long chats I had with Johnny when I was a little boy kneeling at his feet in the front room in Abbey Street when Cassie Ann was at bingo and my daddy in Gormley's or Broderick's pub. I leant forward to lift the pipe and nearly dropped it. For a split second, I thought it was hot to the touch. But it wasn't lit. It was just a wee message from Johnny.

I could feel my eyes fill with tears as I stood there for a long, long time thinking of our Johnny. I still have that pipe of his until this day. Our Johnny and his flaming pipe will always remain within my abiding memory of him.

The Fire

It was around 2 am on a freezing wintry night in late January when Cassie Ann's worst nightmare began. And Abbey Street was lost forever.

I was eight years old when the uniformed RUC police officer burst into our bedroom. We had no idea what he was doing when he picked up me and my younger brother, one under each of his hefty arms, and ran down the blazing stairs and out onto the ice-covered streets. He gently placed us on the footpath opposite, patted both our heads, told us to stay put and then returned to the raging inferno to fetch the rest of my family and the lodgers. In a strange sort of hypnosis, the two of us watched as our house, and those adjacent to it, burnt to the ground. Doherty's, the local undertakers, with the empty coffins and no corpses was the last of the premises to catch fire. When the flames were eventually extinguished, our house and the remainder of the street, were but a mere pile of smouldering rubble. And lost memories.

As we stood barefoot on that frozen street, holding my younger brother's hand, it seemed as if I was having a bad dream which was impossible to be woken up from. Flames mixed with flecks of snow, or possibly ash, dancing across the collapsing rooftops and lighting up the pitch-black sky over Abbey Street. People were running everywhere, buckets in hand, shouting and screaming, lights flickering on and off in the houses opposite and a Catholic priest standing in the middle of the road saying some random prayers. If only he had the mind to bring along a bucket of Holy Water, he might have been some use. Kitty McWilliams, a close friend of Cassie Ann's, who lived closed by, picked me up in her arms, held me tight and told me not to cry. I wasn't crying. I was mesmerised. There was too much commotion and excitement, especially when the volunteer firemen arrived astride their ancient fire engine. By the time they had rolled out the hoses and linked them to the water pumps, all the houses were by now a raging inferno. Sparks from the flames, like angry fireflies, flew randomly across the rooftops and up into the sky illuminating the pitch-black darkness of that night. Eventually, the burning roofs began to collapse, like glowing dominos, immediately causing the few firemen on the street to hurriedly back off until all the roofs had finally fallen inwards onto what remained of the houses they once shielded. Tears were now streaming down my cheeks. I could taste the salt in them as they flowed into my gaping mouth, out of which came not a word, not a scream. Just disbelief and terror on my frozen face.

In the aftermath of the fire, after the pandemonium had died down slightly, I couldn't locate Cassie Ann or my father. They were nowhere to be seen. It was bewildering as I remembered seeing Felix a little earlier, so the assumption was that he went looking for Cassie Ann and would eventually come to fetch me and I would soon wake up in our bed beside my younger brother. It didn't happen. Instead, neighbours gathered up us little ones and we were carted off to their respective houses where we were looked after until our parents could be traced.

The following morning was freezing with flakes of snow billowing across the streets in a bitterly cold easterly wind. Paddy Gallagher, whose house I stayed in, walked me down Castle Street towards the scene of the fire. The street where the inferno had occurred had disappeared. No houses, not even a wall remained, just rubble and an acrid smell of burning furniture. In the near distance, I saw a bareheaded Felix, a man never seen without his cap, holding the old ginger tomcat with badly singed hair under his arm and just shaking back and forth. He might have been crying but possibly not, as Felix was my father and he was too tough to cry. He then proceeded to gently step through the still smoking debris looking aimlessly for whatever he could salvage and, occasionally, he would bend down, cat still in his arms and sift through the ruins and bits of rubble. Every so often he would pull out what looked like a half-burnt photograph or a picture frame with no content and just shake his head. I called out to him but he waved to Paddy for him to take me back to his house, which he did, eventually. I felt incredibly helpless and sorry that morning for a father who was a gentle giant of man but was powerless in the face of such a tragedy. His loss was just as much as that of Cassie Ann, and the rest of his family, and for the remainder of his life he would bear that burden of failure.

After what seemed like days, possibly weeks, I was eventually reunited with Cassie Ann in Mrs Gallagher's front room in Castle Street. She appeared much older and nervous since the last time I remembered seeing her. She wore her horn-rimmed glasses at an acute angle, and behind them I could barely see her eyes peeping though narrow slits. She had the look of fear, and a hint of bewilderment, and her face was stained with what looked like dried blood mixed with soot and dirt. Tears were constantly streaming down her cheeks and her once rich and lilting voice had taken on a deep croakiness, caused no doubt by the smoke inhalation. She frightened me.

I just looked up at Cassie Ann and started to weep. She was different now. No longer the funny, laugh-out-loud, gregarious Mammy who could make a room full of neighbouring women drop there their false teeth into their laps or their cups of extra-strong Barry's tea, with her outrageous stories followed by uproarious, wet-the-knickers laughter. She now resembled a distraught and very frightened soul who had just lost everything that she had once held so dear. Cassie Ann was not the Mother I had known only a few days or weeks earlier. On that terrifying January night in Abbey Street, she lost everything in the fire, including for what seemed like many years afterwards, her mind. It was to be a long time before I saw Cassie Ann again. Years later I discovered that she had retreated to bed in Kitty McWilliams' house and remained there wrapped up in blankets for many weeks before she could face the world again.

The rusting aluminium pish-stained bucket was located at the end of my bed. It was used as the shared receptacle into which we would relieve ourselves during the night. Mind you it wasn't just always pish that went into the bucket. Summers were the worst, especially when we had the occasional warm evenings and nights. The smell of the stale urine would linger in the night air and smother all other relatively pleasant smells coming from the street below.

The impoverished local council did not have the luxury of emergency properties, so until a suitable dwelling was located, we stayed with neighbours. I was housed with the Gallagher family, who had three sons and very quickly became part of the family in their comfortable house in Castle Street. James Gallagher, the father of the house, had been imprisoned without trial by the British in the 1950s for his Republican sympathies and upon his release from a prison ship moored in Belfast Lough, he spoke only in Irish. His hatred for all things British grew as he aged, even down to the tea he drank. Barry's Irish tea was always preferred to Typhoo even though both emanated from India. I always enjoyed listening to James Gallagher blathering away in my native language, although I barely understood a single word he uttered. He, and a distant relative of my mother's, Jim McWilliams, a schoolmaster in the local Catholic Primary School, had been arrested in their homes and taken directly to the infamous Royal Ulster Constabulary interrogation centre in Belfast. There they were questioned at length and tortured by representatives from the security services. They had no access to legal representation and were never put on trial in front of a court of law. Although no charges were brought against them, both men were interned for indefinite periods in the prison ship within sight of land. It was a long tortuous time before they could set foot on land again. James never forgot nor forgave his captors for such vile, inhumane treatment.

Eventually, a house was found for us by the Parish Priest, Father McDowell, also known as Doctor McDowell, as he had a Doctorate in Divinity, that also explains why he never had a stethoscope around his neck. The house, or hovel to be more precise, was in Brook Street, one of the poorest and most deprived streets in the town. There was a brook alright, as implied in the name of the street, but babbling it was not. For those residents living adjacent to the brook, it was a convenient receptacle for offloading the detritus of the night and more often used for disposing of any household waste including dead mice. An open sewer really. During the long summer days, and warm evenings, the children of the street would happily play and occasionally fall or slip into the rat-infested fetid stream and on occasions take a sip or two from the polluted water. But as nobody told us it was that the water was dirty, we went ahead anyway and played in the muck and shite without any worries. Mind you, there were many cases of diarrhoea in the street on numerous occasions.

The dwelling that we were allocated was located at the far end of Brook Street. There were five of us ensconced in one tiny bedroom, the main bedroom. My two brothers slept in an oversized single bed opposite the parents' double-bed, whilst I slept on a heavily stained mattress on a tiny iron bedstead tucked into the bottom of the brothers' bed. There was no room for a wardrobe, nor drawers of any size, so clothes, for what few garments we possessed, were discarded on to the floor or left hanging on the end of the bed. Occasionally, Felix would hang the clothes on the nails hammered into the back of the bedroom door, but it was the floor that was usually the most convenient place for them.

The sheets on the bed were made from old flour bags that my mother had purloined from the local co-op and somehow managed to fashion them by hand in such a way that a rough covering was created for each of the beds. These coverings, or sheets to be kind to her, took time to soften and when washed they provided a degree of comfort. But they were still as rough as a badger's bum.

The second-hand blankets were provided by the local Saint Vincent de Paul and augmented with my father's and his generous friends' work overcoats that provided extra warmth during the cold winter nights. On those nights when it was bitterly cold, we might have the use of a couple of stone hot water bottles that were scalding to the touch and would require wrapping in an old towel before being placed in the bed. Often however, the neck of the bottle would leak and the spilled water would very quickly freeze around the nether regions during the early hours. Waking up with a damp patch around the arse and your tiddly was not much fun. In such cramped conditions, there was little room for privacy with the result that Cassie Ann's depression intensified and she grew remote from us even though we were within touching distance from her restless body and tortured mind every night. Each evening before I fell asleep, I would hear her sobbing as she prayed to Our Lady in Heaven to help her and her family. Countless Hail Marys and novenas were recited in between sobs but Our Lady was obviously too busy those days and nights as there was very little help coming Cassie Ann's way for all her beseeching and praying.

In an even smaller room next to ours, lived our permanent lodger from Abbey Street, Johnny, 'Kirk from Dunkirk'. He had resided with us since the end of the Second World War when he returned from Germany and after the fire there was nowhere for him to live but with us in Brook Street. The big-hearted and equally big-bosomed Cassie Ann came to Johnny's aid and took him in after a fortuitous knock on her door one cold afternoon. His room had a back wall that had partially collapsed so my father erected an old tarpaulin that he had picked up on his travels around the farmyards and fixed to what remained of the wall in an effort to keep out some of the biting cold wind. Johnny had suffered much greater hardships during his internment at the hands of the Germans and was grateful to Felix for his ingenuity. Johnny became our permanent lodger and remained with us in Brook Street during those dark days as an integral part of the family.

The house was in near darkness even during the summer months. The front room ceiling was flaking from the damp seeping through the walls and was lit by a 60-watt bulb. The light it threw out was barely enough to read the few second-hand books provided by the school. Not much homework was ever successfully completed resulting in yet more daily beatings from the Christian Brothers. The scullery was so small that even the proverbial cat would have had difficulty being swung around it. A cracked white enamel bucket with a wooden handle sat in the corner with water filled from the outdoor tap the previous evening. This water was used for washing the plates and cups, and when dirty, the wastewater was handy for washing the stone floor in the scullery with a long-handle mop. In the absence of Cassie Ann, the sister took on the burden of trying to cook and wash clothes and the weans, but for the most part us boys just remained unwashed and profoundly filthy.

The walls in the yard at the rear of the house were crumbling, and in places, parts of those adjacent to a public footpath called the Pads, a shortcut running parallel to the house that led up to the primary school and the Sacred Heart Church, had partially collapsed. However, it was an adventure playground for the boys and girls of the street who would climb back and forth over the high walls without any fear of falling. On occasions, usually at dusk in the late summer, groups of young children from Brook Street would sneak across the manicured lawns in front of the Parochial House and attack the fearsomely protected apple orchard owned by the men in long black tunics known as the Christian Brothers. There always seemed to be a Christian Brother nearby reading his bible, or more likely the racing pages of the Sporting Life, whom we suspected was the appointed guardian of the orchard for that evening. If he was young and had good eyesight, we would abort the apple thieving mission, but if the Christian Brother was ancient or there was no guard, we would raid the orchard, stuff our faces and fill our pockets with the near-inedible crab apples. And a few minutes later throw up on the manicured lawns on the way home.

Occasionally, we would be seen by Hanna on her late evening rounds looking for leftovers after the evening meals. Everyone had dinner at lunchtime, and in the evening, we had tea, so the ever-astute Hanna was always on the lookout for scraps of food left over from that evening's feasting of bacon and bread toasted on the open fire of the front rooms up and down the street.

"Have you weans nothing better to do but rob the good Brother's orchard?" she would bellow from her toothless mouth. She liked the kitchen of the Christian Brothers as their leftovers were much more superior than those of all the neighbouring houses in Brook Street.

"Get home with yous or I'll be telling your Mammies," she would shout after us as we scampered away from her knowing full well that she could never catch us.

33

"I know who yous are, you wee skitters, and don't be giving me any cheek do yous hear me?"

But she never told our Mammies, as she probably thought it quite funny and daring of us to raid the Christian Brothers' orchard. She was always wary of them, and in later years she confided to me that,

"They are a shower of tight auld drunken bastards." Hanna was a great judge of character and she certainly would have had no qualms about saying what she thought. I never plucked up the courage to disagree with the inimitable Hanna.

Across from our house was the smallest street in Ireland, St Michael Street. It consisted of only one building, a large house that was split into two dwellings. The rear house was inhabited by an aged husband, who was blind, and his devoted wife, who took care of him and their home. They had a long garden stretching all the way down to Brook Street in which his wife had planted with vegetables and nurtured with a multitude of flowers, especially roses, geraniums and jasmine, a resplendent array of abundant flowers that bloomed in the summer months and enriched the surrounding streets with their scents. There were numerous smells in Brook Street, mostly unpleasant, but on rare occasions the fragrance of the roses and jasmine from St Michael Street would waft down from the garden and fill the night air with such sweetness that the stink of the pig shit and the open sewer could be forgotten, even if it was only for a few short hours.

This new temporary home for us, temporary meaning just over five years, was adjacent to a long and winding, tree-lined avenue that led up to the imposing Parochial House. This was the stately residence of the Parish Priest and his cohort of curates, all paid for by the impoverished parishioners, many of whom resided in the shacks and hovels in the street below, almost within spitting distance. The vast landscaped area in front of the Parochial House, constantly tended and manicured by underpaid local gardeners, was out of bounds to those unwashed, lice-riddled scamps from the surrounding area. But we ignored the threat of a good hiding from the priests to enjoy swinging from the trees and throwing sticks up at the chestnut tree in early Autumn to dislodge the nuts so that we could play conkers with them.

By way of respect, and sometimes fear, my father would doff his cap each time a priest would drive out of the avenue, and in return, if he was fortunate enough to be seen, he would receive a casual, almost royal, wave from the busy cleric. But not always. I used to think that Felix resented the well-to-do priests but he was a deeply religious man and had a grudging respect for their role in society.

Across from the Parochial House where so many self-inflicted male young virgin clerics lodged in great comfort, stood a magnificent convent belonging to the Sisters of the Loreto Order. From the early 19th century, the Loreto Sisters had developed as a distinct community in Ireland. Their founder was an English Woman, Mary Ward, who was instrumental in creating convents across the world with the Loreto convents ultimately establishing themselves as some of the most highly regarded places of education for young women from the ages of 11 to 18. Neo-gothic in style, the imposing building was erected in 1855 and towered over Brook Street where the town's poorest could be found. The cavernous building was home to countless novices and fully-fledged nuns, all of whom wore the full-length habit consisting of a black tunic covered by a scapular and a cowl with a veil.

The nuns took vows of obedience, poverty and chastity, but living so close to young Catholic curates housed within knicker-throwing distance, was always a challenge. There were two types of nuns. Sisters who looked after the house and gardens and making sure that the Priests' vestments were washed and cleaned on a daily basis and Mothers whose function was to educate the young girls in all things academic and Catholicism of course. After taking their vows the nuns would assume male names such as Mother Oliver, Mother Kevin or Mother Francis Paul whilst the Sisters just held on to their own Christian forenames. Over the years, several young nuns and weak-willed curates fled together from their respective and highly restrictive careers and eventually married, much to the consternation of the Parish Priest and an incandescent Mother Superior. The convent also encompassed a grammar school for girls, some of whom boarded with the nuns during term time. This made the convent a babe magnet for the unwashed, spotty-faced local boys, who would climb the steep rough walls surrounding the entire convent during late evenings to see if any of the inmates were in desperate need of their unwelcome company. The girls would indeed have had to have been truly desperate given the state of the potential smelly Casanovas, but nonetheless we persevered with our endeavours to woo a couple of the boarders. Sadly, the impetuous sex-starved youth were usually thwarted by a cane-wielding, nimble-footed novice, who would delight in viciously whacking any audacious brat on the back whom she could apprehend and would lay into him with her cane across his rear end as he attempted to climb the steep wall to escape.

The grounds of the convent were manicured to perfection; with lawns that were tended daily by low-paid gardeners from the surrounding area. When a nun happened to wander past a gardener busy tending the roses, he would be required to stop what he was doing and show his cap to her as a sign of respect. More likely, it was the fear of being sacked for being insubordinate. There were several tennis courts and even a netball court where the boarders would play to an audience of keen-eyed, randy little giggling boys hiding in bushes behind the oak trees at the far end of the lawns. The hope was to catch sight of a pair of yellow bloomers under the extra-long brown skirts worn by the young females as they leapt towards the netball hoop. Many young lads in the street would spend sleepless nights thinking of the various moves on the netball court that they had witnessed earlier in the evening, even if the female participants were wearing extra-large yellow, knee length knickers.

When on the rare occasion that Cassie Ann was feeling a bit better, she would come down from the bedroom and take a seat in the corner beside the open fire in the front room. Her world had collapsed and her health, both physical and mental, had suffered. Cassie Ann would appear distracted as she sat gazing into the open fire as the blocks of wood crackled and the burning coal emitted thick black smoke into the tiny room. Her face was now thin and gaunt with streaks of grey running through her wild unkempt hair and her eyes no more than tiny slits of purple and red from constantly crying. Having suffered so much in her early life, she had eventually found happiness with Felix, a kind and loving man and at long last found a home that she could call her very own. One greedy, reckless neighbour who thought it a great plan to set fire to his shop to claim the insurance, instead burnt the entire row of houses to the ground resulting in homelessness and misery for so many. His greed and the firestorm that followed left Cassie Ann devastated and broken. She would recover; it would take time but she would be her, smiley, noisy self again.

It was Felix who had the unenviable task of transporting the communal bucket down the stairs every morning the contents of which were disposed of in the outhouse. This privy, or bog as my father referred to this repository for shite and pish, was not that private as the roof and sides were peppered with numerous large holes and gaps, thereby open for all passers-by to gaze down upon us as we relieved ourselves. The outhouse was situated in the back yard between the nettles and the dock leaves and located as far away from the house as possible, thankfully. It was a rusting, tin-covered contraption of a latrine with an ever-present odorous stink that resembled the remains of the rotting corpses with long dead creatures. When walking towards the toilet rats would suddenly scurry away into the crevasses in the wall between our dwelling and the yard next door that housed the pigs owned by the occupant, the eccentric Hannah Shannon. It was no way to have your daily pish and shite.

The Brock Lady of Brook Street

I was about 8 years of age when I first encountered the Brock Lady, as she was known around the streets and back lanes of the town.

Hanna was a rotund little toothless woman who seemed to waddle rather than walk. No matter what the weather—snow or sun, Hanna always wore a headscarf knotted under her chin and was a formidable sight pushing her brock barrow as she approached you on the footpath. Hanna gave way to no man, no woman nor child and certainly no clergy. Even the Parish Priest would be inclined to stand aside when she was pushing her barrow-full of food waste at full pelt down the street. She had precious little time for those collared bible-thumpers other than the excellent quality of food that they discarded from their nightly dinner table.

In every respect, she was an enterprising little powerhouse who knew what she wanted and invariably got it.

Every afternoon, as regular as the proverbial clock, Hanna could be heard and seen trundling along the street with her contraption of a brock barrow made from an old wooden box with long wooden handles perched on squeaky pram wheels shouting,

"Have yous any brock for me the day" she would squeal.

Her outward appearance was one of intimidation but once she had your trust and confidence, she was a heavenly creature with numerous tales of the rural community and the many varied and eccentric individuals whom she had encountered during her lifetime. She came from a farming background in deepest Tyrone, and the fact that she was living in a town, did not deter her from raising pigs for profit. There was no husband and certainly no love interest and I never had the courage to ask why love had never entered her life. However, there was an adopted daughter called Sarah Jane; and together with the pigs, that was the extent of Hanna's little family.

Brock is a local word for food waste which, in Brook Street, was the remains of that day's dinner, or lunch if you happened to be posh. Mind you, there weren't too many posh people in Brook Street at the time. Hanna would collect the various potato skins, discarded vegetables and remnants of meat and bones and would add them to her barrow to feed to her pigs who were never particularly choosey about what they ate. Seldom did she smile, but if the takings were plentiful, a full sight of her darkened gums would be displayed.

Hanna kept pigs in her back yard of a terraced house next to her little dwelling and these creatures were her only means of financial survival in an impoverished 1960s community. The number of porkers she kept was determined by the size of her yard, which was not substantial, so there would be the occasional crowding and subsequent screaming from the animals because of their proximity to one and other.

She obtained the piglets from local farmers and fed them to a suitable size after which they would be collected by a friendly driver from the local branch of the Ulster Transport Authority and driven to the abattoir in Cookstown for unceremonious despatch. There they would be converted into bacon and sausages and any other products a pig could provide. In effect, Hanna had her own little pork production plant which was both self-sufficient and profitable.

Her brock rounds took her to Castle Street, Brookmount, Derry Road, the local convent and the Parish Priest's house on the hill. The quality of the discarded meals and rubbish would be more fulsome than those of her near neighbours in Brook Street. Refusal to contribute to her brock box could be met with a fierce gurning of the gums that would frighten the local women and many a man as well. It paid to be friendly to Hanna.

We lived adjacent to Hanna's house, once an old military hospital that comprised of three floors upstairs and numerous downstairs rooms that led off to an enclosed backyard where the pigs resided. How she came to possess the house, no one seemed to know, but she certainly made full advantage of the space provided. Living in that squalid house next door to Hanna, the first sound I would hear when I awoke each morning was the noise of the pigs grunting and squealing in the yard next door looking for their breakfast of leftovers and anything barely edible.

On that first morning in our new abode, I leapt out of the tiny bed and ran out into the yard and climbed up on to the whitewashed wall to have a look at the commotion next door. Peeping over her wall, I could see a mass of dirty pink, young pigs scowling and nuzzling each other to get to the brock. I stayed there for ages enthralled by this strange sight until my mother caught sight of me and dragged me off the wall and gave me a kick in the arse as I ran in through the back door. I had the impression that she was not a pig lover.

I was fascinated with our newly acquainted neighbours and could not wait to meet Hanna and find out all about her animals. Her door was always open. So, one morning I walked into her front room which had a stone floor.

"So, you are one of those weans from next door," she muttered through her gums.

"Hello Mrs, I am sorry to be bothering you," I said, while backing off a bit from Hanna.

When I would occasionally visit Hanna, her face would break into a wide gurn. "Well, welcome to my wee house, Son, and you can call me Hanna. They all call me Hanna around here and more besides, I expect." From my very first meeting with the uncrowned Queen of Brook Street I instantly was captivated by Hanna and her toothless gums.

Over the years I got to know more about this eccentric creature, who she liked and trusted and whom she disliked and I learnt so much about her pigs and how she made her money. She would point out which ones were nasty and liable to bite and which ones could be approached to pet. And of course, I would be there at the door to watch the dispatch of the mature pigs to the abattoir and the arrival of the new piglets.

"When you get bigger, you will have to get the hell out of this place, Son. There is nothing here but poverty and hatred, and there will be no end to it. Mark you my words," she growled as she spat some phlegm into the roaring fire after taking a long pull of a Woodbine cigarette.

I used to sit with Hanna as she recited endless stories about the various characters that had lived in the street in the past, not forgetting of course, that she too was as eccentric, if not more so, than any of the personalities that she had mentioned. For a young boy to nestle down beside her open turf fire, watching this engaging woman who had struggled all her life merely to exist, to listen to her regaling me with stories of banshees and fairies and bad-tempered priests, and of the history of the street and its inhabitants who were impoverished through no fault of their making, was to be transported into a world of magic and wonderment.

Hanna raised a girl whose name was Sarah Jane. For all intents and purpose, she was the daughter. The poor girl was not her natural daughter and everyone in Brook Street was aware of the fact, but it was one of those unmentionables that all knew about but didn't discuss especially within earshot of Hanna. Allegedly, Sarah Jane was born on the wrong side of the blanket after an illicit fling in a remote part of the county between two consenting but unmarried teenagers. When Sarah Jane arrived into the harsh world, she was hurriedly transported to Hanna for her to raise as her own. To her credit as a single surrogate mother, Hanna raised Sarah Jane as best she could and life just went on without a word from anyone, including the all-seeing, and occasionally not-hearing, local clergy.

Hanna never bothered with false teeth after she had the last of the rotten ones removed many years previous. She wore thick long socks with heavy black hobnailed boots both in winter and in summer. She was of an indeterminate age, and without her teeth, she appeared ancient, although she was probably a good bit younger than her looks. Her pigs apart, Hanna's one abiding passion was smoking untipped, extra-strong Woodbine cigarettes, one of which could be seen constantly dangling from her thin lips as she guided the brock barrow along the roads, lanes and footpaths of the surrounding streets. Her use of the English language could, at best, be described as unique. On her daily tour of the streets,

Hanna could be heard swearing and cursing profusely. No one was exempt from her wide range of profanities, all delivered whilst smoking a butt of a Woodbine between chapped lips whilst aggressively pushing her brock barrow past unhelpful or deaf neighbours.

"Nosey bitches, the lot of them, Son," she would often say to me with no reason other than to annoy any onlookers.

"They should all just mind their own stupid business," she would continue in between taking another drag on her cigarette.

"Mark you my words they would want to know when you had a shite last. I wouldn't trust a one of them."

I so enjoyed doing the rounds with Hanna and her brock barrow. There was never a dull moment when she was in full flow of bad language and invective.

She always kept a spare half-smoked snig of a Woodbine lodged behind her left ear just in case she ran out of cigarettes, or fags as she referred to the weed, during her rounds. Once relit, a half-smoked butt would induce fits of coughing and a swift clearance of the lungs with a full-blooded gob from Hanna onto the footpath. She seemed to really enjoy the quick buzz from the relit half-smoked cigarette as if the onset of a good cough was a pleasure. Her pigs had to be fed, and neither man nor woman, or even cheeky children, would stand in her way.

Hanna would always stop at a little shop at the end of Brook Street to have a yarn, or a good auld gossip as she would say, with the two spinster sisters who ran the small, dimly lit emporium nestling on the corner of Brook Street and Abbey Street. The ladies were known to the neighbours in the street as the Two Nancys, although only one of them was christened Nancy, and nobody really had a clue as to the first name of the other, the smaller and quieter of the two. The shop sold a limited selection of groceries and sweets, the latter kept in tall jars that usually consisted of Pear Drops, Dolly Mixtures, Bonbons and Bazookas, all of which could have been residing in the dust covered jars for many years. Penny Chews with green and white wrapping were available from a small box located on the narrow counter located between the two resident tom cats who objected to being disturbed, especially by customers. Nancy the Elder sold cigarettes to all and sundry with no questions asked about age or gender. They could be bought in packets of 10, or even packets of 5, and if a man was hard-up, he could buy a single cigarette that Nancy was always happy to sell to her captive, and ever grateful but constantly impoverished customers. For those discerning neighbours in Brook Street who enjoyed the infrequent luxury of cheese, Nancy sold Irish Cheddar that she would carve from a large block that she kept covered with a stained teacloth on the back shelf. After giving the blade of the knife a quick wipe on her heavily soiled apron, Nancy would cut off a large chunk of cheese from the block and would wrap in a piece of brown paper and then accept payment. Nancy's cheese was my first introduction to exotic cheeses as it contained several layers of blue that might well have been mistaken for Stilton, although mould may have been a more accurate description. The Nancy Emporium, as some of the locals referred to the shop, was not so much a shop rather more a meeting place for those who had very little money to spend but had plenty of time to linger and chat about all manner of happenings in the world.

Every few months, my father's pig lorry would arrive at the front door of Hanna's house for the collection of her fattened pigs and their final journey to the abattoir in Cookstown and their premature departure from the world. The squealing creatures would be grabbed simultaneously by their floppy ears and curly tails and manoeuvred from the back yard, through the interior of the house, out the front door and loaded on to the back of the vehicle that would transport the screeching creatures to their date with a dinner plate. The intensity of their squealing sounded as if they were aware of their impending fate and were trying to object but to no avail. Pigs are clever creatures. They have good long-term memories, and they can be socially manipulative with other pigs. They can tell which people are nice to them and which aren't. Therefore, when the time came to throw them unceremoniously onto the back of a lorry destined for the abattoir, it was not a surprise that they put resistance. Bacon and sausages are a staple diet of Irish folk with pigs a necessary requirement in the food chain and the Brock Lady of Brook Street was the perfect provider. She was indispensable in so many ways.

After a good cleaning and disinfecting of the yard coupled with the disposal of the mounds of putrid pig shit into the brook, or elsewhere, a task given to Sarah Jane, it was time to repeat the process of rearing, feeding and disposing of her squealy pigs. A week after the collection of the bacon-ready pigs and their short journey to Cookstown, another lorry would arrive. A fresh consignment of wriggling piglets would be offloaded and carried though the house and jettisoned into Hanna's backyard, there destined to begin the short cycle of feeding, nurturing and eventual slaughter. This was Hanna's world.

Young Tilly, short for Matilda, Noble, lived in one of the tiny houses opposite ours. She was a slight woman with an abundance of intelligence but a paucity of education, who would occasionally help me with my homework. She was kindness personified. As with all the families in the street times were difficult. Although Tilly's family had precious little, she was generous with what few items of food or clothing she possessed and would share with others if she thought they were in greater need. Each week, representatives of Saint Vincent de Paul, a Catholic charity, would visit families who had little income and were desperate for food and clothing and would provide them with enough essentials to see them through the week. If the men from the charity thought that the family were in dire financial straits donations would be made to the neediest, and if Tilly received some of this charity, she would send me down to Nancy's shop for ten Woodbine, most of which she would eagerly smoke in front of the open fire in her tiny front room. It was with the help and persistence of Tilly, a bright intelligent woman, but lacking the opportunity to receive a decent education that would have served her well in later life, who helped me pass the much sought after 11-plus exam and my subsequent entry into the big bad world of the Christian Brothers.

Food was scarce in Brook Street particularly fresh food. Fortunately, Felix worked for the local transport company, where he and his colleague and best friend Jim, would drive to farms across the county to collect animals for slaughter. This gave him the opportunity to pick up bags of spuds, cabbages and other vegetables from farmers with whom he became friendly and as a family we were much better off than our neighbours in the fresh food department. To supplement our varied diet every Friday morning, a thin little man wearing a tattered flat cap would push a handcart on wheels through the streets selling fresh fish scattered across the top of his cart and would loudly announce his presence.

"Fresh herring, fresh herring, herring alive. Get them now whilst they are sleeping and cheap." This was Billy McBride, who managed a roaring trade in his definition of 'fresh' herring. Other fish such as salmon were expensive and out of the reach of the pockets of those who lived in the street, but herring was cheap and plentiful. Before buying the fish, Cassie Ann would occasionally quiz Billy about the freshness of his product to which he would reply whilst putting two fingers to his lips and whispering:

"Would you be quiet, Mrs, if you raise your voice you will wake them up, they are that fresh."

Billy was a popular little man in that small town and every Friday his 'Herring Alive' would echo around the streets, much to the amusement of the local children who would follow him and his handcart in their droves. It was because of Billy that we had herring for dinner every Friday, a day when the consumption of meat was forbidden by the Catholic Church. Cassie Ann would over-fry the herring on a pan over the open fire in the front room and then dish them up with some boiled spuds covered in butter as an accompaniment. The challenge of the meal was to find a way to eat the herring without choking on the multiplicity of bones contained in the damned fish. Billy might have been a popular local personality but his fish were less so.

The years quickly passed and my teenage years were on the near horizon. Eventually, our family moved away from Brook Street and its cast of wonderful, generous and funny characters who had so little but gave so much of what they had to each other. I still remember sitting on the little three-legged stool beside the open turf fire and watching Hanna light her untipped Woodbine cigarette from the packet of five, and after a few coughs, she would spit with great accuracy into the flames of the turf fire and commence yet another long-winded story with which to beguile and entertain me.

I think of Hanna from time to time. Her pushing that contraption of a trolley full of stinking kitchen waste around the streets of the town shouting, "Have yous any brock for me, the day?"

Hanna frightened many a soul but little did they know that her heart was large and full of goodness. I, for one, will never forget the Brock Lady of Brook Street.

Nobody Told Us We Were Poor

To wipe our arses in the latrine or bog as my older brother would refer to the outdoor loo, Cassie Ann would cut up pieces of old newspapers into neat little squares that were then attached to a long metal hook by the side of the toilet bowl. These improvised bum wipes, not exactly the Izal of their day, also had several unintended uses not least the opportunity to catch up on the local news albeit in snippet-form only. A quick read of the obituary section followed by a wipe of the arse after defecation was not an unpleasant way to pass the obligatory time in the toilet. The downside, of course, was that this type of bum wipe was so rough that it served merely to spread the shite around the lower orifice rather than cleanse the bottom. For reasons best known to herself, Cassie Ann insisted that we use only the torn remnants of the local Protestant newspaper, the Tyrone Constitution, to wipe our arses. Not for her the risk of using the pages of the local Catholic newssheet, the Ulster Herald, where there was always the distinct possibility of a picture of a Catholic priest or a respected dignitary ending up with our shite all over their gurning faces. Their shitty days would eventually arrive without any assistance from our arses.

Winter mornings were a constant challenge. There was an open coal fire in what was called the front room which served both as a living room and a sitting room. It was here that Cassie Ann, if she was well enough, would bake the soda bread on a griddle hung over the flames and hang a large black pot of potatoes on a long hook attached to a bar across the inside of the chimney. Preparing and lighting the fire in the open grate was a morning ritual. Us young ones would be required to tightly roll old newspaper sheets and knot them so as to form the basis of the fire. The knotted paper briquettes would be set on fire using Bryant & May matches or from a lit candle and when the first flames began to glow a full sheet of a newspaper was held over the face of the grate. This was to provide the 'draw' whereby a flow of air up the chimney would assist in helping to ignite the paper and sticks. The one downside was the paper used in creating the flow would regularly catch fire resulting in a panic to stamp it out on the stone flooring. And then start all over again.

Before bedtime, Felix would back fill the fire with slack, a combination of cheap wet pieces of coal that would form a cushion or blanket over the flames which, in turn, would keep the fire alive until morning when it would be replenished with larger pieces of dry coal. Every Friday, Gerry the Coalman would arrive in his open-back lorry to deliver a couple of bags of loose slack and a hundredweight of coal which he carried on his back through the hall and discharge into a large wooden container outside the backdoor in the yard. Gerry was a generous little man. In addition to his usual deliveries, he would invariably drop off a sack of broken pieces of wood and sticks for use in making up the fire during the freezing cold Winter mornings. There was never a charge for this largesse.

The first task of each day was to chase and flatten as many as possible of the countless cockroaches that engulfed the kitchen floor. In their hundreds they would appear during darkness in pursuit of slivers of food and form a moving black mass of insects. Cockroaches are omnivorous scavengers that spread diseases and bacteria and will happily eat each other and their own droppings if nothing else is available. These nocturnal insects would suddenly scamper in all directions after the overhead light was switched on first thing in the morning. At the first sign of light the creatures would make a mad dash for the warmth and relative safety of the grate before we could trample them all to mush on the stone slabs of the kitchen floor. It was a never-ending battle between the insects and the infants with the latter just about winning. Cockroaches make a strange popping sound when their shells are crushed and a red-like blood substance would ooze out from their flattened carcases. Most likely it was a batch of eggs that the cockroach carried beneath its abdomen that would cause the bloody mess, and the unbearable stink. Cockroach killing was just a game for us. But for Felix, it was a daily ritual of using a mop to clear away the blood and entrails of the trampled cockroaches.

For the children of Brook Street, the start of a typical day was the killing spree of these little creatures followed by a hurriedly eaten slice of bread and jam, a quick wash in the outdoor concrete job box, if the weather was not too cold, and off to school at the Christian Brothers. Another day of learning by rote, constant and often brutal indoctrination in the Catholic faith and daily reminders that we were fortunate to obtain a good schooling even though we were continually reminded that we were both stupid and poor. Toothpaste, toothbrushes and the cleaning of teeth were considered a luxury and the reserve only of those people who lived in the nice houses on the other side of town. Cassie Ann and Felix, both had all their teeth removed by the dentist in their forties and wore false teeth, or choppers, for the rest of their lives.

Most evenings before sleep the parents would immerse their respective sets of false teeth in a large jam jar filled with water and a Steradent tablet that was used to cleanse the false teeth. The principle being that as if by magic the tablet would make the false teeth sparkle when worn again in the morning. However, it was not unusual for my mother's lower false teeth to appear by accident in my father's mouth first thing in the morning. After a quick inspection and a wipe, they would happily exchange them without any discussion or fuss. Teeth that you were born with were in short supply and the vast majority of adults developed the skills of using their hardened gums to eat all manner of food, whether it was meat or spuds, without the aid of dentures.

If there were illnesses, and there were many in that poverty-stricken street, local remedies were often called upon to cure the patient. Placing raw potato slices on foreheads to cure a headache was popular, ear infections cured using vinegar poured directly into the area infected, rubbing menthol on a chest to help open it open but the best medication of all was the cure-all of all ointments was Black Ointment. This was a solution sold by the pharmacist in a small round cardboard box that would be used on a multiplicity of illnesses. There was no need to bother the doctor if Black Ointment was available. All skin irritations including pus-filled boils, burns and any skin rashes would be healed with a generous application of the miraculous restorative contents of that little round box. There were no labels or instructions on the box that described what went into the mixture but every house had a supply in case of minor, and the occasional major, emergencies.

For young children, Brook Street and the surrounding fields and lanes was a huge playground. Not far from the street was the local train station, busy all day and night delivering goods and animals to and from outlying villages. It delivered the milk and bread early each morning, carried passengers long and short distances and the railway employed many people who had worked all their adult lives for the company. The line through and from our small town in the West of the North of Ireland was finally abandoned as a result of a decision based on findings by Doctor Richard Beeching, the Chairman of British Railways. He became a household name in Britain in the early 1960s for his report, The Reshaping of British Railways, commonly referred to as 'The Beeching Report', which led to far-reaching changes in the railway network, popularly known as 'the Beeching Axe'. He deemed that trains in our part of the world were unnecessary and therefore had to be closed with lots of job losses The rural areas, the villages and small towns that depended heavily on a regular train service, were left with no other option but to use lorries on the inadequate roads to take their goods to the markets in the major towns and cities. Doctor Beeching was from the Isle of Sheppey in Southern England and never visited our town to see the enormous benefits of maintaining the railway. It was the lifeblood of the community and its closure left a gaping hole in the local transport system that has never been filled.

Sadly, those annual day trips on the steam train to Bundoran, and the glorious Atlantic beach in Donegal, which were once such a pleasure, were no more. From now on it was the fume-filled bus on the first Sunday of August for the one-day pilgrimage to the seaside and that lung expanding breath of sea-fresh air followed by a quick paddle in the freezing cold Atlantic Ocean.

But when those steam trains were shunting back and forth to the railway station, they would pass under the narrow bridge at the top of Brookmount, belching out volumes of dark grey smoke that would engulf the watching children who would be looking down from the bridge above as the locomotives made their journeys to Derry and Strabane and elsewhere. It was a time of mystery coupled with unbridled joy for dirty face children who did not mind being covered in the coal dust that was being pumped from the long funnels on the steam trains as they roared past under the bridge. Children would gaze in wonder at the trains approaching from one side of the road and then hurriedly run across to the other side to watch as the train slowly disappeared into the far distance, travelling to some far-off exotic destination. Belfast most likely.

On the far side of the bridge that overlooked the railway tracks there was a steep grassy knoll that was used as an improvised slide by the youngsters, both boys and girls, during the warm summer months. When there was a drop of rain or drizzle, the Slippy Tits, as they were known to the locals, a stream of shrieking kids would take turns to slide down the wet slopes, the arse of their shorts quickly being covered in brown mud. Squealing and shouting, they would take turns to slither fearlessly down the steep incline stopping just short of the rail tracks and any approaching trains. Then a quick scramble back up the muddy slope to await another turn. It was only after a few years that I eventually found out the real meaning of the Slippy Tits, the expression that we were so fond of saying as youngsters actually referred to women's boobies but the memory of those carefree days on the greasy slopes beside the now defunct railway tracks never left me.

In the absence of any sports equipment in the surrounding area games were improvised by the local children with Kitty Out being one such game. To play this activity there was a requirement for two pieces of wood, a short piece shaved to a sharp point at each end and a longer thin piece with which to use as form of miniature bat. The short one would be angled on the edge of the kerb of a footpath and when hit with the larger one, it would fly into the air and whoever caught it would then use it to attempt to knock over that larger piece of wood that had been placed at an angle leaning in front of the kerb. This nonsensical game would amuse the local children for hours on end and would be played on the main road where cars were a rarity and the children safe from any harm. Usually. Then there was Blind Man's Bluff where a child would have a piece of cloth tied across the eyes and he or she placed in the centre of a group of squealing young ones with the 'blind' child attempting to catch and identify the victim through touch. It usually ended in tears with the 'blind' child tripping and scratching the hands or face of some unfortunate youngster.

Trees were in abundance—especially on the grounds of the Parochial House. Chestnut, oak and cherry trees and even an enormous money puzzle tree, standing as if on perpetual guard at the front of the imperious priests' house, that bemused everyone when seeing it for the first time. It was exotic for the location in which we lived but we never did see any monkeys trying their luck in climbing the tree. The winding avenue leading to the grand house on the top of the hill was tree-lined with lawns closely cut and trimmed from early spring through to late autumn. This was a privileged area for the sole use of the not so humble Catholic Priests who could occasionally be seen walking around the grounds in quiet contemplation or very possibly reading the racing pages of the Irish News or the Daily Mirror. Cherished grounds such as these were not for the unwashed young barbarians from the street below to engage in football thus tearing up the pristine turf or the use of makeshift go-carts with which they would spoil the aesthetic beauty of the well-tended lawns and spotless driveway.

In the early evenings when the Parish Priest and his curates were dining, and almost certainly imbibing decent wine, groups of young boys and girls from the surrounding streets would converge upon the private grounds and scamper up the trees, especially the chestnut ones during early autumn when the nuts were ready to fall or be knocked out of the tree by sticks used as projectiles to loosen those still clinging to the branches. Ascending these precious trees was strictly forbidden and those caught in such acts of wanton vandalism would be subjected to a thorough beating from the guardians of the lawns, the priests. But nimble young hands and small feet made the task of clambering up and over the trees look simple especially for those who could hang precariously from the branches whilst reaching out for the plump nuts, almost but not quite, out of reach of the grasping hands. At every opportunity during that period of dusk when the clergy were gorging their faces and drinking their fill, the branches would gently sway under the weight of so many eager, unwashed but happy, little children. Swinging from branch to branch and invariably falling on their arses onto the soft pristine lawn below was always a risk but one worth taking for a handful of precious chestnuts. There was always a lookout though. One child, usually the one who had a fear of climbing tall trees or the youngest, would remain vigilant with eyes peeled for any sign of a black cassock in full flow emerging at speed from the big house on the hill with the aim of capturing one of them and the inevitability of a good thumping. When the curate was spotted, the shout went up and the children, much faster than any drunken curate, would scamper in all directions and eventually make it to a place of safety where the conkers would be counted and shared out in readiness for the games the following day.

"I know whose yous all are you wee brats and if I get my hands on any of you there will be hell to pay," would shout the tipsy irate curate as he watched the young scallywags fleeing in every direction. From memory, men in frocks never did succeed in catching anyone but at Mass on the following Sunday morning it was always best to avoid eye contact if that pursuing curate was the Celebrant and had good eyesight.

One bright summer day, a young priest arrived in the Parish who was different. Unlike so many of the other prayer-pumping preachers this priest was different. His name was Father Shields who even had a first name—Seamus, rather than just Father, and he was unusual in that he seemed to be a man who enjoyed engaging with the local youth. He must have been brought up in an orphanage or parachuted in from some distant mission or planet because he was certainly not cut from the same clerical cloth as those other individuals purporting to be one of Christ's representatives on earth. Dapper in his clerical suit and wearing horn-rimmed glasses, one of Father Shields' first acts shortly after his arrival was to introduce the local youngsters to a game of football. He opened a previously inaccessible walled-off field at the bottom of the parish lawns that backed on to Brook Street and instructed the gardeners to cut back the long grass to create our very own football pitch. Temporary goalposts were set up using long bits of wood that he had been scrounged or scavenged from somewhere behind the Parochial House and with his jacket hanging from a nail on the fence, but still wearing his clerical collar, he commenced the first of many games of football with the great unwashed youngsters of Brook Street. He even had the decency to call us by our Christian names—something a priest would never do, except at a Baptism or Confirmation and then with great reluctance. The good Father very quickly became hugely popular with everyone who attended at the Sacred Heart Church and even went so far as to reach out to the local Church of Ireland Minister who worshipped nearby. And the wee man, he was not tall by any stretch of the imagination, was just brilliant at Confession. You could tell him any old pack of lies and all the penance you would receive is a few Hail Marys. And no prostrating yourself in front of the altar either with all those old Biddy Pish Wishers watching and praying for you to go straight to Hell for your sins without even ever having had a decent snog with a girl from the Protestant community. Incidentally, the term 'Pish Wishers' refers to the noise old women make when they recite their prayers, usually endless Hail Marys that they keep count of on the well-fingered Rosary Beads. The sound that emanates from their narrow lips resembles a 'pish wish' effect. As if summoning a cat.

Father Seamus, as he was known during his stay in the Parish, reinvigorated the faithful by creating social platforms for people to meet and have some fun for a change, instead of constantly having to listen to sermons on how bad we all were and that Hell was just waiting for those who strayed from the path of righteousness. During May and October, Jesuits used to descend upon the town and preach from the pulpit about the wickedness of man which was fine except for those sex-starved young lads who would nearly kill for some of that wickedness. They did not want to hear about wickedness and debauchery, the local young men just wanted some of that forbidden action especially if it involved fiddling with girlie bits. Father Seamus was not into all the ranting and raving about sinners, especially when there was so much poverty and misery within his congregation. He may well have been a man of the cloth but his aim in life was to bring some light relief and joy to the suffering of the people whom he was charged with looking after. He introduced pantomimes for adults and children and arranged for their production in the local town hall, a place usually out-of-bounds for so many poor people. For a couple of hours each evening the audience at these events could forget their poverty and endless struggles and laugh at the shenanigans on the stage.

Pantos were a novelty and people flocked to them in their droves, especially as tickets were sold during the interval for prizes that would make any poor family happy and of course fill the coffers of the Church. Father Seamus was not a selfish man. He could see that the many of his congregation were impoverished and he made every effort to plough back any profits into the community providing he had the permission of the Parish Priest. Local men and women would be persuaded to build stage props, arrange and take part in auditions and musicians would be encouraged to give their time for free for the short duration of Cinderella or Goldilocks and the Three Bears. For a few nights each year local men, who would normally be seen as macho, could be seen on stage wearing women's clothes, their rough manly faces smothered in overkill make-up, playing the part of the Ugly Sisters or Widow Twanky and none would think it anything other than good family entertainment. At the end of an evening's performance, the audience, well-off and poor, would return to their homes but for those few hours their lives would have been transformed by a little light entertainment with which to forget the daily grind of their existence and simply enjoy the nonsense on the stage of the Town Hall care of Father Seamus.

"That is some cough you have there, lad. You'd need to get that seen to or it'll be the death of you. Probably all those fags you're always smoking," was a common exchange between men that would frequently be heard on the street. Unfortunately, for many souls it was more likely that it was consumption, or TB as it was more frequently known. Consumption was the layman's succinct name for the disease; graphically describing the effects of untreated tuberculosis —the victim 'consumed' by weight loss and breathlessness. It devastated the lives of thousands across the island of Ireland with no respect for man-made borders. Spitting, for years a national past-time in Ireland, and if it was an Olympic sport, the Irish would be regular gold medal winners, proved a ready source of flying bacteria and helped spread the disease.

TB

It could lead to meningitis in young babies, and often fatal, spread rapidly amongst the poor where one child would develop the decease followed by a brother and then his friend a few doors down the street and very quickly an epidemic ensued. The only form of recovery was many months of isolation in a sanatorium in a remote part of the country where the patient, if fortunate, would eventually survive. The treatment consisted of no physical activity, total bed rest, two bottles of Guinness daily if an adult and not teetotal and plenty of nutritious food. During the daytime, patients would be encouraged to put their heads out of the windows of the sanatorium and fill their lungs with fresh air. Hospital beds were often wheeled out on to verandas regardless of the season so that the patient could see daylight and breathe in the oxygen in the cold air. TB was rampant during the 1950s and 60s and took many lives with more Irish youngsters slain by the disease than had died in the two World Wars. Eventually in the early 70s, TB was all but eradicated, but not before many people perished or survived with weakened lungs and a perpetual cough. It was the silent killer that few discussed in public for fear of it visiting upon them or their families.

Several young people from Brook Street would just simply disappear for many months, or sometimes years, and would return with gaunt features and severe weight loss confirming what disease they had been suffering from and where they had been for so long. TB was indeed the hidden killer of so many innocents.

A Mother Once Again

Although she had numerous relapses, after a few years in the house at the bottom of Brook Street, Cassie Ann eventually and very gradually regained her health and became a mother once again. Her body grew much stronger and her mind finally found some solace. She had returned to us. One Friday evening when Felix was permitted to indulge in a few bottles of Guinness after a gruelling week driving the pig lorry, he brought home a very unexpected but much welcome present. A black and white television set. It was not a new one but it was a real working television set. He had a little win betting on the horses and after making the down payment he was able to make the instalments on hire purchase from Hynes, an electrical shop located in the centre of the town. Cassie Ann took one long look at the small contraption and shook her head.

"I've heard about those things from Mrs McCullagh. She says they are a total waste of money and there is nothing worth watching anyways. Mark you my words, nothing good will come from having that thing in the house. Give me Radio Eireann any day and that lovely Michael O' Heir," she announced to us and the neighbouring children gathered in the front room with mouths wide open gazing in anticipation at the blank box now resting on a small table in the corner.

"It'll be good for the young ones," replied Felix, ever the diplomat.

"Especially when it's bucketing with rain outside," he continued; his eyes desperately avoiding the glare of those of Cassie Ann.

"Be it on your own heads. That's all I'm saying. There is the Devil in that thing," she mumbled as she turned and marched into the tiny kitchen at the rear of the house.

After Felix eventually managed to obtain a signal with the little aerial balanced on top of the set, we watched some programme about the hunting of wild animals in Africa. In black and white of course. The giraffes appeared to have black and white stripes, and the lions looked a sort of grey around the edges, especially when they ran after some frightened-looking water buffalos with their long horns. Still, it was something to pass the time when the evenings were cold and some of us were recovering from whooping cough or a bout of pneumonia.

Then one night, Felix announced that his all-time favourite American actor, whom he would have loved to have met, was to appear on the television later that evening and we could all sit in the cramped front room and watch it together. The film was *The Quiet Man* starring John Wayne, the Hollywood superstar whose actual name was Marion Morrison. It was a story about a giant of a man of Irish parentage returning to his roots from America where he was a once famous boxer but with a secret past and was now looking for peace and maybe some love in rural Ireland. Just like Felix, who had lived in the Bronx and Queens New York for a few years but returned to his roots in his beloved but impoverished homeland. Although Felix had spent only a few years in the States following his return he was always referred to as the 'Yank' in the village where he was born. As the film commenced the front room was packed to capacity with neighbours and their children seated on the stone floor or standing near the open fire all gazing at the small box now perched high up on the top of two overturned tea chests, one on top of the other, that Felix had acquired from the local co-op in George's Street opposite the Catholic church.

From the opening scene to the very end the *Quiet Man* had the assembled Brook Street audience transfixed. The film had everything that would appeal to Irish and American audiences. Drinking, fighting, religion, greed, horses and the love of a good woman for her cigarette smoking hero. The Director was John Ford who, together with John Wayne, was best known for Westerns most of which were shot around Monument Valley in Arizona. Ford had directed over 140 films but The Quiet Man was the pinnacle of his achievements and won two Academy Awards in 1953. Mary O'Hara, who was born in County Mayo, was the love interest and had the music of the film played to her during the final hours of her long life when lying on her death bed. Felix was mesmerised by the acting in the film and during the famous fight scene he could be seen moving his arms and shoulders as if he was part of the action. Cassie Ann had initially refused to watch the film but eventually sat on a stool near the front of the crowd and at the end her heavily stained apron was used to blow her nose and possibly to wipe away a tear from her eyes. When asked by Mrs Noble what her thoughts were on the film, she simply replied, "Ach, it was alright I suppose." She had a broad smile on her face, though.

Brook Street was a veritable hotbed of gossip, what with sins of the flesh and the mind in great supply. Strange noises would emanate from inside the back doors of some of the houses as we sat with friends throwing stones at the rats scurrying around the fetid water of the brook during those long hot summer evenings. We were too young to understand what these strange noises represented but there was a never-ending supply of new babies arriving on a regular basis, so something interesting must have been happening behind those thin walls. Children were a vital commodity for the Catholic Church and Brook Street was a veritable breeding ground for new entrants to the faith. There may not have been much food and money was forever in constant short supply but there was room for us children to play and no end of wild adventures to be had.

Nettles seemed to be everywhere near that rat-infested putrid brook. If one of us was stung by the plant thereby causing a painful burning sensation, the remedy was simply to grab a mature dock leaf, of which there was a plentiful supply growing around the not-so-babbling fetid water and rub the leaf vigorously over the infected part of the body. Worked every time with almost instant relief and no call to be running to your Mammy who would probably give you a quick slap across the back of the head and boot you out of the house again. A favourite pastime in the summer was the hunting for rats' nests. On those occasions when we discovered a nest, we would ensure that the parent rats were first bludgeoned to death with heavy sticks, or a hurley stick, known in Irish as a *camán*, as rats had a reputation for attacking youngsters, when threatened. When the nest was exposed, up to 50 young rats, surprisingly known as kittens, could be seen squirming, their pink bodies with eyes closed. The older lads would gather bits of dry straw and a few sticks and use a long thin piece of wood with a burning rag attached with which they would set fire to the nest having first thrown some paraffin over it. The younger ones would squeal and laugh as the sound of the burning baby rats popped in the fire. Of course, no mention of these activities were ever raised during Confession as we did not think it sinful to burn such creatures and besides the Priest might not think it a terrible thing to rid the street of such vermin.

During late December, when we were on the Christmas break from the daily indoctrination by the thugs at the Christian Brothers school, and when there was snow lying on the ground, the young boys of the street would use my father's leather apron that he wore when shepherding the pigs out of the back of his lorry into the waiting arms of the executioners at the abattoir as an improvised sleigh. Flakes of snow falling like some great white armada from outer space, covering the pristine lawns and gardens of the Parochial House was a perfect invitation for the infant vagabonds to make the most of the weather knowing full well that

56

even the most resolute cleric would think twice about chasing the shifting shadows of smelly miscreants. With a long piece of cord attached to each side of the front of the apron, two boys at a time would take turns sleighing down the snow-covered grand avenue of the Parochial House. Naturally, other boys would keep watch in case Father Clerkin, the mad cleric with the pointy nose, would suddenly appear and beat the living daylights out of any child he could apprehend, which was rare. But he and his pals in their stiff white collars would seldom venture far from their drinks cabinets and roaring fires to chase light-footed skinny young hooligans across their precious lawns. The fact that the avenue led directly on to the street below was seldom a risk to the young snow revellers as there were very few cars in the district, and if one happened to come slowly motoring along, it was a risk worth taking. The more snow the merrier, as were the participants on the leather apron sleigh run. Many injuries occurred, usually minor, but mercifully nothing serious.

Baths and bathing were rare in most of the houses in Brook Street. There was a tin bath in our house but Cassie Ann had her own problems to worry about and having to wash filthy weans regularly was not one of her priorities. Occasionally, my Godmother, Emma would visit the house and would insist on filling the tin bath with warm water and scrub each of us in turn. It felt great to be clean on those rare occasions and drying oneself in front of the open turf fire in that tiny front room, but Emma had nine children of her own and her hands were more than full so the opportunity of a hot bath was rare.

Brook Street was one of the poorest areas in the town. It was populated with Catholic families who eked out a living on very little income but their generosity to each other was a testament to how they lived their lives. One prime example was the Hamilton family. They were poor and struggled to bring up their children on the meagre wages of the father of the house. On his way out of the house to work one crisp winter morning, he very nearly stepped upon a basket that was placed outside the front door. In the basket was a new-born child whom he instinctively lifted and brought into the warm kitchen where his wife immediately took control.

Many questions were asked about the parents or family of the abandoned child but no knowledge of the mother was ever forthcoming. There was nothing for it but for the child to be adopted and even though the Hamiltons had very little to feed an extra mouth, Mr Hamilton, whose one luxury in life was the daily habit of smoking his pipe, gave it up so as to help pay for the upbringing of the new addition to the family.

In the years to follow that child grew up to be a renowned singer and entertainer with a massive following from teenagers all over Ireland. He was known as Sean 'Speedy' Hamilton whose rendition of 'The Land of a Thousand Dances' by Wilson Pickett became his trademark song.

Brook Street was indeed a street of heroes in so many ways.

A Sunday in Bundoran

When she was up and about and herself again, Cassie Ann would insist on treating us to the annual outing to Bundoran some 35 miles away in County Donegal in the Irish Republic. The day would start with 10 o'clock Mass in the Sacred Heart, of course, followed by a rounding up of the youngsters and off to the depot with everyone excitedly piling into the bus that would transport us to that land of magic beside the sea.

To reach that enchanted place beside the Atlantic Ocean, there was one major obstacle to overcome. The heavily fortified and armed to the back teeth army and police patrolling the border crossing at Belleek situated between Fermanagh in the North and Donegal in the South. The Customs Post, staffed with British soldiers and members of the RUC, straddled the narrow road leading to the coast and ensured that a smooth, uninterrupted crossing was never going to happen. Bus drivers always allowed extra time for the long wait as the soldiers stood by or hid behind sandbags with their rifles cocked and ready as if World War III was about to commence in the back of the rusting old bus with Bundoran as its destination on the front. The armed policemen, sidearms visible with the occasional sub machine strung over the backs of a couple of them, would walk up and down the inside of the overcrowded vehicle packed with the holidaymakers and question those whom they thought looked in any way suspicious. Admittedly, most of the menfolk on the bus did look a bit suspect but not in a terrorist way, rather more like men who required a good night's sleep and a couple of bottles of stout and a few large whiskeys inside them. After the much-anticipated delay and the names of several men methodically scribbled into the notebooks of the RUC officers, eventually, the bus would continue its slow journey through the town of Ballyshannon, and past the sparsely populated Irish Army barracks at Finner Camp and onwards to our final destination, the long golden beach front of Bundoran by the wild Atlantic Ocean.

Bundoran was a small seaside town nestling in the distant shadow of Ben Bulbin, sometimes spelt Benbulben, which could be seen in the distance in nearby County Sligo and not far from where W B Yeats was laid to rest. During the winter months, when the fierce winds whipped up by the Atlantic Ocean would blow continuously, Bundoran was home only to the hardy locals residing in the town. Come late April and May, the town would once again come to life and visitors from all the neighbouring counties, and even as far away as Scotland, would descend upon the town's cheap boarding houses and caravan sites to take in the fresh sea air, to wallow in the seaweed baths and to over-imbibe until paralytic drunk most evenings in the town's many drinking establishments. Young men and women from farms in Tyrone, Donegal and Fermanagh would descend upon the many dancehalls in the town many of them looking for romance and perhaps a husband or a wife, or at the very least, a suitable partner that they could have a few dances with before the evening ended. The major showbands of the day, with their mix of country and western music and current trends, would play to packed halls at the weekends when couples would meet, mix, drink and dance until the early hours. If lucky, a bit of snogging and sand in your shoes on the beach afterwards. A weekend in Bundoran was the highlight of many a farmer's daughter or son.

During the height of the troubles, many 'on-the-run' IRA men and women would hide out in any number of official and unofficial drinking establishments in the town under the watchful gaze of the local Garda, or police force, big men renowned more for their brute strength rather than for the overwhelming brilliance of their intellect. Because of its proximity to the border with Northern Ireland, and the multitude of remote crossings that were seldom patrolled, the IRA would send small groups of their men to attack RUC barracks and army patrols along the border with Fermanagh and Tyrone in the North. Once their attacks were concluded, they would scurry back over Laghy Mountain, through Pettigo and into the relative safety of the Republic of Ireland again. Bundoran was not just a gathering point for active members of the IRA and its many sympathisers but a hub from where many operations were planned and launched.

For almost two centuries, people had flocked to the beach at Bundoran especially on hot, and even cold, summer days, of which the latter was more prevalent. The long beach is called *Trá na Draina* (the strand of the strong) where families such as our own would congregate and spend the afternoon eating homemade sandwiches of corned beef and tomato, drinking strong tea and enjoying the occasional rays of sun in between frequent showers.

"Right, you boys get yourselves into your togs and go for a paddle in the ocean. It'll be good for your circulation," Cassie Ann would command as soon as we had made ourselves comfortable on the sandy beach. For each of us she would hold up an old towel with which to hide our dignity as we changed into our 'excuse for swimwear' and occasionally let the towel drop so that she and the neighbouring women could laugh hysterically at our youthful embarrassment.

"Sure, he has nothing to be showing the world just yet, that wee boy of yours, Mrs," would scream Mrs Fullerton, seated next to Cassie Ann, both of them with their false teeth clacking as they struggled to keep them in their mouths between fits of laughter.

"Off you go now with the rest of them and have a paddle in that ocean. But not too far, do you hear me?"

The fact that her father had died as a result of a drowning accident nearby did not deter her from allowing her boys to play in the water. None of us could swim, however, so we never ventured too far into the breaking waves. The togs, or more aptly thin excuses for swimming shorts, seemed to be of a knitted material, that as soon as they became wet, would stretch down to our knees under the weight of the seawater. For some unexplained reason there was always a small pocket sown into the inner part of the pants. Presumably, it was to keep your spare change or valuables both of which none of us possessed. Paddling in the cold ocean waves was not pleasurable and every time an exit was attempted, the roar from Cassie Ann would go up,

"Get back in there and enjoy yourselves," just as our toes and fingertips started to turn a dark shade of blue. There was more chance of catching pneumonia in that freezing ocean than acquiring a suntan. But if she insisted on us 'enjoying' ourselves, then who were we to disagree.

Meanwhile, the husbands and fathers would have made their excuses and left the women to look after the weans on the beach and would venture off to Frank O'Neill's pub in the main street where they would spend the best part of the afternoon and early evening drinking Guinness and singing their heads off with friends whom they would meet on that first Sunday in August every year.

Bundoran, and paddling in the ocean beside the silver strand, was one of the few escape days for Cassie Ann. With all the worries and fears forgotten for a few precious hours Cassie Ann could relax with her family and her friends and neighbours on that Donegal beach on the first Sunday in August. The following day—Monday, would be the start of another year of scrimping and scrounging for herself and her youngsters and her ongoing struggle to recover from the mental trauma brought about by that fire in her house in Abbey Street.

Nuns

Cassie Ann's aunt, Sister Martha, was in the Order of Loreto nuns. They were also known as The Sisters of the Immaculate Deception by the girls whom they taught and the local lads who they were forever chasing from the convent grounds. Mother Theresa of Calcutta, who was of Albanian and Indian origin, was also a member of the Loreto Order and was subsequently elevated to Sainthood by Pope Francis for her work with orphans in India and elsewhere. Sister Martha, who hailed from a tiny farm in remote Donegal, was still awaiting such an elevation when she passed away. Martha may not have achieved sainthood but she was a very devout and wonderfully kind woman whom Cassie Ann adored.

Nuns are a rare breed. The definition of a Catholic nun is a woman who lives a contemplative life in a monastery or convent which is usually cloistered (or enclosed) or occasionally semi-cloistered. But when a nun is promoted and becomes the boss, she is referred to as 'Reverend Mother' or 'Mother Superior'. It is she who is ultimately responsible for all the activities of the convent including the safekeeping and education of the girls who attend and board within the convent building. Saintly Sister Martha was one of those nuns who had taken solemn vows and lived in the convent, or cloister, and said prayers using an outsize pair of ornately crafted Rosary Beads that only those who had taken Holy Orders would use. But in between prayers, Sister Martha had to slave away her days in the laundry washing and ironing the vestments that the Parish Priest and his curates wore to Mass and Confession. She had the responsibility of washing their shirts, socks and messy underpants as well.

When I was six years old, Cassie Ann took my hand and walked me up the tree-lined winding avenue to the Convent and up the steep steps where we eventually stood in front of an elaborately designed heavy oak front door. After ringing the bell, we had to wait until an aged maid eventually opened it and quietly enquired as to our business at the Convent. The maid spoke in such a low voice that it was as if there had been a recent death of one of the occupants and she was required to whisper.

"We're looking for Sister Martha McGread, Miss," said Cassie Ann to the septuagenarian maid in a voice loud enough to waken any slumbering nuns within the convent.

"I'm her niece if you must know. And she is expecting me. This is the letter that she wrote to me recently," remarked Cassie Ann. I looked at the letter and wondered why Sister Martha would write to her niece who lived only a couple of hundred yards away and then looked up at my mother who winked ever so slightly in my direction.

"Come in here now and just take a seat over there on the chairs for a few minutes while I go and find her for yous," said the maid as she turned and silently tipped-toed away over the highly polished ornate tiles covering the passage that led into the furthest depths of the Convent. She gradually appeared to shrink as she seemed to take forever to reach the end of the long and overly decorated hall.

After what felt like an age, a small figure materialised in the distance. It was ghost-like in appearance and was slowly floating towards us as if on casters or invisible tiny roller skates. She appeared not to have any feet. The apparition seemed to glide in our general direction and eventually arrived in front of us. To a six-year-old boy, it seemed like a vision of the Virgin Mother descending from Heaven. It was not of course. The vision gradually morphed into the shape of a smiling little nun who was wearing her full-length habit and a veil covering most of her round face. She spoke in a very soft, almost angelic, voice which surprised me. Sister Martha greeted Cassie Ann with a gentle hug that was reciprocated, a small gesture that I had never witnessed before from my mother or since. My mother was a country woman and hugs were alien to such a breed of Irish women. Hugs were only for new-born lambs and baby calves who had lost their mothers at birth.

Tea and dainty little cakes and buns were delivered to the side room by the aged maid where the two women chatted for ages, with me sitting in the corner stuffing my face with the cream buns and listening to them but not understanding what was being said. Cassie Ann was proud that she had an aunt in The Sisters of Loreto and would drop it into the conversation with her neighbours at every opportunity. When the time came to depart the convent, Sister Martha escorted us to the massive oak front door that she eventually managed to pull open. Just as we were saying our farewells, Sister Martha produced a miraculous medal from deep inside her cassock which she handed to me and then produced a strange cloth-like object that she gently hung around my neck. Cassie Ann later informed me that it was called a Holy Scapular, which was composed of two small pieces of wool cloth and an inch or two of square wafer-thin connecting strips. It was to ward off evil but it never seemed to work for me in the years ahead. As Cassie Ann nudged me to thank Sister Martha for her kindness, the nun delved into one of the deep pockets again and produced a banana. Having never seen one before, I was perplexed what to do with it so I gave it to Cassie Ann who, on the way home, proceeded to unpeel it and with a broad grin commenced eating the fruit.

That was the first and last time that I ever saw Sister Martha. She died a few years later when Cassie Ann was not at her best. That little angelic Loreto Sister was laid to rest with other deceased nuns in a graveyard behind the Sacred Heart Church. My abiding memory of her will always be that of a cloaked vision descending from Heaven who gently glided around the Loreto Convent on tiny roller skates and who always had a ready supply of bananas.

Derry Road

Felix was eventually made redundant from his job as a lorry driver delivering fresh pork, aka pigs, to the abattoir in Cookstown. Cassie Ann immediately took responsibility for the redundancy money Felix had received from the company and promptly decided to buy a terraced house on the Derry Road that had recently come up for sale. The house was a two-storey dwelling with a closed-in yard with a door leading to a long garden at the rear. It was just perfect for Cassie Ann. The major attraction, however, was not the garden but an indoor toilet. Five years of having to use an outdoor loo was now well and truly behind us and the pleasure of a having a shite in a warm room without spectators was to be marvelled at and to be enjoyed. No more hauling of buckets of water across a freezing back yard to dispose of your waste. In the future it was simply a case of pulling a chain, the water miraculously appears and your business simply disappears down the toilet bowl and into the waste pipe. And no more rats to worry about either.

It was as if Cassie Ann was reborn when we moved into that old house on the Derry Road. A fully functional toilet beside a large bath with two taps, hot and cold. During those first couple of days in that house we took turns constantly flushing the toilet and running the taps in the bath just to see how they worked.

"Varicose veins or not, I am getting into that bath this evening," she roared when she first set eyes on the cream-coloured tub, "now find the switch for the hot water tank and put in on. I need plenty of warm water."

When she saw the long garden at the rear of the house for the first time, she put her hands to her mouth and gasped. She had spent years dreaming of her very own garden and now she was the proud possessor of one, a long empty space in which to grow plants and flowers to her heart's content. Her first thoughts were for geraniums, hydrangeas, roses and any other flowers that she could plant. Felix had other ideas that included planting potatoes, cabbage, carrots and broad beans. They eventually compromised. Top half for flowers and bottom half for vegetables. It turned out to be an excellent compromise.

There was even a black Bakelite telephone on a small shelf in the hall. It was huge, cumbersome, and very probably one of Alexander Bell's prototypes. We took turns to pick up the receiver to hear if there was any noise coming from it. My sister suggested that we should ring somebody to announce to them and the world that we had moved into our new house and that it had its very own phone. The only obstacle was that we knew no one who possessed such a means of communication and hence the Bakelite remained untouched for many months. The ever-resourceful Felix eventually found the telephone numbers for the Parish Priest and the local doctor and wrote them on a piece of paper that he stuck on the wall above the telephone. Heaven and health in that order, of course.

Number 12 was the middle of three terraced properties directly facing the British Army barracks on the other side of the road. This was a heavily protected, sprawling encampment occupied at the time by a regiment of the 16/21st Lancers. St Lucia Barracks, to give its proper title, was leased from a local landowner in 1860 for the princely sum of £60 per annum on a 999-year lease and was the original base for the Royal Inniskillen Fusiliers. The permanent presence of a major British Army battalion was not reassuring to many Catholics, although there were some benefits in that it provided menial, low-paid jobs for local men who had weighed up the risks of working for the Army. Poverty always overrides pride.

Derry Road was one of the main thoroughfares in and out of our little town and was in constant use by traffic during daylight hours. The ultimate destination of the road was Derry, or Londonderry, as our Protestant neighbours would refer to the city, up in the Northwest of Ireland. The City of Derry was both ancient and very beautiful but it was a troubled place with deep-rooted bigotry and discrimination within its medieval walls. It was in that city that the Civil Rights movement would eventually take shape and would change the very governmental structure of the Six Counties of Northern Ireland.

Derry, known as the Maiden City for reasons that were never clear to any of us, straddles the River Foyle, the fastest-flowing river in Europe. For a naïve young 16-year-old with bad acne and a dreadful haircut it was a fascinating city to explore. In 1689, the Catholic James II of England and Ireland and James VII of Scotland, laid siege to the walled city, which was at the time a Protestant stronghold. The Siege of Derry, as it became known, was the first major event in the Williamite War in Ireland. The inevitable massacre was initially foiled when 13 Protestant apprentices shut the gates thereby creating the siege which lasted for 105 days until relief eventually arrived in the guise of troops loyal to the Dutch King William of Orange who sailed up the river in a flotilla of warships. Each year, in early December, Orange bands parade around the City Walls followed by sash-wearing members of the Apprentice Boys, not all of them in their youth, commemorating the famous victory over the Catholic King James. The defeated King eventually died in exile in 1701, a broken man.

Protestant and Catholics seldom lived in close proximity to each other in our thinly populated small town and as a result so little was known about each other's culture, lives and aspirations. The girls at the Protestant Academy were attractive but totally out of bounds to us lecherous, unwashed teenage Catholics. Not only would the clergy frown upon such liaisons but our families, especially the mothers, would take great umbrage at the thought of their precious sons or daughters having a relationship with those from the 'other side'. It was certainly rare to encounter friendship from the 'other side' but occasionally a bond would be made and sustained. One exception to the non-mixing rule was the Mann family who lived in a nearby housing estate and were just one of those rare departures from what was considered the norm. George, the father of the house, was an ex-soldier with a disability, married to a local Protestant woman and who lived happily surrounded by Mass-going Catholics.

There were many offspring but there was one son called Ronnie personality shone bright from an early age. His birth name was Ronnie but to all his friends he was known as Blackie as he was known to all and sundry because of his jet-black hair. He was a far too good-looking young lad, who owned a beat-up old jalopy of a car that was big enough to carry multiple passengers. At every opportunity he would round up those young men who fancied a bit of an adventure and off they would go in search of music, dances and girls, especially girls. All the girls loved Ronnie, and he was no shrinking violet when it came to repaying that affection. He possessed a smile that would charm the birds out of the trees, and more specifically the two-legged ones at the local dances. Blackie was a few years older than most of us but he had no qualms about shoving us all into car and drive to Derry with us young ones crammed into the back seat. During the Summer months this was his routine. A crowd of lads with Blackie as the leader and off for a bit of an adventure in that boisterous city on the River Foyle. After safely parking the car Blackie would wander around the streets, his disciples in tow, and would chat up numerous girls who were themselves looking for a bit of stimulation especially with handsome young lads from elsewhere. Invariably Blackie would strike lucky early on and take his leave of us with the finest looking young lady. After an hour or so he would return, his face aglow and off we would go on the prowl again. Several of us younger ones thought that there was always an opportunity to move in on one of Blackie's discarded young ladies but my luck was always out just like the pimples on my nose. We were never jealous of Blackie. Not in the slightest, the good-looking, smooth-talking, girl-pulling bastard. On the return journey from Derry, usually well after midnight, he would stop at a café outside Strabane., It was a well-known haunt that stayed open into the small hours to serve food to late night girl hunters such as ourselves. Blackie was usually the only member of the crew with money and he would buy large bags of greasy chips and distribute them amongst his youthful pals in the back seat. He was a real hero to us spotty boys in so many ways. We craved his company and envied his charm and his ability to chat up so many girls. Just a few short years later, Blackie died in a head-on car crash on a country road. The good really die young as they say in the movies. Blackie was certainly one of the good guys and it matter not whether he was a Protestant or a Catholic.

Our neighbours were Catholic, apart from a few souls including a very portly, unmarried gentleman who owned a little grocery store nearby. He also sold petrol at exorbitant prices but that was a product that was never a necessity in our household since the possibility of my father owning a car was some way off. This kindly gent, who went by the very un-Catholic nalme of Kenneth, was a member of the Jehovah's Witness but kept his religious beliefs to himself. And besides Jehovah's weren't really Protestant according to Cassie Ann. Ken, for short, lived in a large, rambling house nearby and would let out rooms for rent to single ladies of a certain age in order to augment his income and thereby help to sustain his weekly contribution to the Church of Jehovah. He was a jovial man with a broad smile and a willingness to help and would even et neighbours have provisions 'on the tick' in order to make sure that there was always something for the children to eat when they came home from school. He was reimbursed when money was available but would never chase for any outstanding debts. He should have been a Christian but he was too kind and too considerate to be one.

Cassie Ann soon made the run-down property a home for her youngsters, or weans as we were often referred to. Young boys in these parts were called 'cubs' and young girls known as 'cutties' and collectively children were called 'weans', presumably from the weaning of babies when nursing. The expression is not dissimilar to 'bairns' in Scotland. Mothers were always referred to as 'Ma' or 'Mammy' and the father as 'Da'.

Cassie Ann loved having the neighbours sitting with her in the kitchen most days of the week except Sundays when attendance at Mass was compulsory on pin of excommunication. In those Sunday afternoons there would be many visitors, relatives, friends and neighbours with the kitchen booming with music blaring out of the ancient radio broadcasting from Radio Eireann in the Irish Republic. Cassie Ann was a great radio enthusiast and enjoyed listening to the BBC news at 1 pm from London read by the well-spoken Scotsman, Alvar Liddell.

"Hold your tongues," she would say to whoever was within earshot in the kitchen as the news started, "the BBC News is on."

"Bong, Bong. Here is the News at One from London read by Alvar Liddell. Bong, Bong."

"He has a great voice, that Al Waddy Dell," was her daily reminder to us all of just how much she enjoyed listening to the presenter's deep, slightly Edinburgh accent.

Once I had the temerity to inform Cassie Ann that her 'Al Waddy Dell' as she called him was a man whose actual name was Alvar Liddell. She glared at me with those eyes that could stop a herd of rampaging bullocks and promptly berated me for such bad manners in front of her neighbours.

"You call him whatever you like, cub, but to me and all my neighbours, he is Al Waddy Dell, do you hear me?" she pronounced with great solemnity whilst looking around at the other nodding women in the kitchen for approval. They all approved.

Cassie Ann's regular visitors all seemed to suffer from a vast range of medical complaints. There was always a great desire to provide in-depth details of the latest ailment with the other ladies nodding in agreement at whatever disorder or affliction was raised. A bad bout of varicose veins was usually the number one complaint amongst the assembled ladies. Whoever's turn it was to disclose their malady would always insist on showing whatever leg was the worst affected by pointing out the various lumps and bumps so that the other women could gaze intently and then compare.

"These veins are killing me. Would you just have a look at the state of them," said Sadie who lived in one of the Jehovah's rented rooms three doors down the road.

"Oh, sweet Jesus, they are bad enough now Sadie but have a wee look at these ones," would come the reply from Mrs Fullerton whereupon she would take centre stage whilst simultaneously hiking up her long skirt.

"Have you ever seen the state of these legs? Too many bloody weans and now that is all there is show for it. Varicose bloody veins and no known cure. They have me tortured."

"You can get them drained these days if you can get the doctor to give you a note for the County Hospital," replied Cassie Ann.

"But these thick vein stockings help a bit though. Bought them from McGread's chemist in John Street and I can swear by them," she went on.

I was supposed to ne revising for some exams or other whilst seated in the corner and would surreptitiously listen to these exchanges but when the subject turned to ill-fitting bras, Cassie Ann would send me to the shop for a pint of milk even though the milkman delivered our milk to the front door every morning.

The kitchen was a hotbed of gossip and frequent updates especially on who was dying or who had died recently and from what dreadful disease.

"She always had a bad heart, that poor wee woman and her with all those young ones to look after," says Mrs McGuigan.

"Aye, and that man of hers never was much use. Would hardly get off his arse and him just lying around the house all day stinking the place out of it," replies Sadie.

"A good-for-nothing right enough and never was anything else," she would go on. And all these conversations shortly after most of them had been to 10 O'clock Mass in the Sacred Heart Church, all except who was of no known religion.

"That Mrs McGonagle one is having another wean. Did you hear? That must be nearly 14 she has already. God love the poor woman. Where do you think they put all them young ones? She only has a wee house up the Gallows Hill," replies Mrs Fullerton.

"Would you read my tea leaves, Cassie Ann?" pipes up the usually very quiet Mrs McSwiggan whose ample arse covered the battered settee that was covered with a throw that had seen better days.

The ladies would all be drinking extra strong cups of Barrys' tea that was brewed in a large tin teapot residing in its permanent slot on top of the range. Because Cassie Ann's father had died before she was born, it was deemed that she had some special gifts or powers, one of which was a cure for the whooping cough, apparently. The story, or myth, went that she could not cure members of her own family but she could cure others by gently rubbing on the affected part of the body whilst saying a few prayers. However, her real claim to fame was that she could read tea leaves.

"Give me that cup of yours when you're finished with it and I'll tell you all about any good or bad luck you'll be having Mrs," she says to Mrs McSwiggan.

After gulping down the remainder of the tea the cup was duly handed over to Cassie Ann who covers it with her right hand, shakes it a few times and then turns it over onto her left hand and looks at the formation of the tea leaves.

"Ah heaven's above, Mrs there'll be a death in the family soon I'm afraid," whilst looking directly at Mrs McSwiggan. The fact that the dear lady's father was nearly 90 years of age and constantly gasping for every breath was never in Cassie Ann's thoughts at all.

"That's shocking. But best to know these things in advance Mrs," replies a despondent Mrs McSwiggan whilst wiping a tear from her left eye with a handkerchief that hadn't seen washing powder for many months.

The reading of tea leaves was a regular occurrence in that kitchen with an audience totally enraptured by Cassie Ann's fortune telling performances. I would sit there completely enthralled by her stories with each of them accompanied by a little vignette and I would gaze at her with a combination of amusement and enormous pride. She was an actress. Occasionally, Cassie Ann would come out with some outrageous prediction and, surprisingly, it would come true. One instance in particular was the name of the jockey on the winner of the forthcoming Grand National, Eddy Harty on Highland Wedding in 1969. Looking into the cup presented by Mrs Fullerton, she announced:

"There may well be a hearty wedding next Saturday Mrs," the day of the Aintree Grand national and sure enough they all had a little punt on the horse which came first and resulted in a considerable windfall for each of them. Mind you, that was the last of her winning tips.

For some obscure reason Cassie Ann's love of animals extended to the acquisition of a budgie. Now where this creature came from and why we were the recipient was always a mystery but there it sat in its cage squawking away from morning to night. It was old and quite manky and never spoke which according to Cassie Ann it could but simply refused to do so. My father claimed that the reason for its belligerence was that it was a Protestant budgie.

The flightless, speechless creature resided in a rusting wire cage in the front room, that place reserved for special visitors such as the clergy or nuns who would make the occasional unannounced, appearance. The bird was always a great talking point for such visitors. Cassie Ann would fuss about how clever and exotic it was and how proud she was to be the owner of such a strange pet. Sadly, the budgie's days were numbered. One of the mad feral cats made short work of the unfortunate creature one evening when the cage door was accidentally left open and all that remained was a scattering of bloodied feathers and a bit if its beak. There were to be no more budgies after the sad demise of dear Joey. Cassie Ann was not best pleased and, unsurprisingly, the suspect cat disappeared a few days later.

A few months into our residency in the new house on the Derry Road, a rumour quickly spread around the town that Queen Elizabeth, the Queen Mother, was to attend a function in the army barracks across the road. The regiment in situ at the time was the 17th/21st Lancers, a cavalry regiment who had no horses but instead drove around in heavily armed vehicles harassing the local young lads at every opportunity. The Queen Mum was the Commander-in-Chief of the Lancers and was to be the guest of honour at some special function to commemorate the Battle of Omdurman where the regiment defeated some nasty foreigners minding their business in their own back yard in far-off Sudan.

The story at the time was that the toilet facilities for Her Majesty were in dire need of restoration that meant urgent work was required to bring the toilet to be used by Her Majesty up to the standard that would be suitable for a Royal bottom. Days before her arrival, local tradesmen were brought into the barracks to erect and decorate a brand, spanking new toilet facility for the sole use of the Queen Mother's bum. On the day of her arrival, a small crowd of nosey locals, mainly of the nationalist persuasion, lined up along the street opposite the entrance to the army barracks and watched as a black limousine slowly drove up to the gates with the Queen Mother alone in the backseat gently giving the royal wave to those watching. Some of us waved back, although Cassie Ann had expressly forbidden us not to be encouraging that sort of nonsense. She stood with her Rosary Beads in her hands reciting a few Hail Marys.

"She's a foreign Queen after all and has no rights here," she forewarned us. Still, we received a little wave in return and a half smile from the old lady who was wearing a large pink hat that made her appear as if she had just come directly from the horseracing at Royal Ascot.

We were aware of her visit to the barracks as the details had been disclosed to those townsfolk who worked at the camp and in no time at all the entire population was updated on the purpose and timing of the visit the Royal dignitary. The Queen Mother, who was reputed to enjoy the occasional sherry, and a large glass of gin or two, was supposed to be on a tight schedule, as was her bladder. The event celebrating the hammering of a crowd of lads in North Africa was curtailed as she had a pressing engagement in some other location and as soon as the dinner and speeches were over, she made her excuses, donned her pink hat, popped into the backseat of the extravagantly long black limousine and departed with a quick wave to the assembled troopers and disappointed officers. The newly built Royal toilet, that had cost so much to erect, went unused and long faces from the Colonel of the $17^{th}/21^{st}$ Lancers and medal-bedecked colleagues ensued. The one benefit was that the regiment had the use of a brand-new toilet for their own personal use in the future, the only downside being that it was painted pink, the Queen Mother's favourite colour. A new loo that was nearly used by a Royal bottom was written in the annals of the history of the town and embellished endlessly especially after a few glasses of Guinness in the local hostelries.

"Not even a pish did the old lady have, not a bloody piddle. What a shame," was the frequent comment when the story of the Royal Loo was ever mentioned in the pubs. The Queen Mum and her unused loo became quite a cult story throughout the land.

One spring Sunday morning, Felix was walking home from 10 am Mass. He was deep in conversation with other Churchgoers as they approached the top of the Derry Road, only to be met by a lone RUC constable standing in the middle of the road. A few passers-by asked the constable what he was doing there especially as he was redirecting traffic in another direction. He advised them that the police station had received a coded warning that there was the threat of a bomb planted in a car outside the Army Information Offices some way down the road. His instructions were to stop any traffic traveling down the road past the suspect vehicle which was clearly visible not far behind the constable. He was on his own and was not capable of stopping large numbers of people from making their way home from Mass so he ignored those who simply failed to accept his warnings.

Felix and his neighbours continued walking past the vehicle parked some 150 yards from the front of our house. As they strolled past the car, the bomb exploded and sent debris and bits of metal flying in all directions. The device may have been on a timer or remotely detonated and was most certainly planted by the Provisional IRA who were at war with the British at the time and the obvious target was the army barracks. The effect of the explosion was devastating. Many people were seriously injured, but miraculously no one was killed. Felix, who was within a few feet of the explosion on the other side of the road where the car was parked, escaped without a scratch. His closest neighbour had his leg blown off beneath the knee. Felix and the young constable used the belt of the police officer's trousers to secure a tourniquet on the injured man's leg in an attempt to stop the haemorrhaging. He survived.

As for Felix, he was totally deaf for many months but eventually recovered his hearing, more or less. The damage to the surrounding properties was extensive and as for our house the roof was blown off. Cassie Ann was now a much stronger person both mentally and physically and hurriedly organised the restoration of the roof and the replacement of the many panes of glass that were smashed by the flying debris. More bombs and misery were to be visited on that little town in the years ahead.

Riots

A baton charge by the police to disperse a group of stone throwers in James Street.

One early spring evening, there was to be a gathering of the Civil Rights movement in the town. Such a turnout was forbidden by the RUC, under instructions from the Stormont Government. There was a directive that nationalists would not be permitted to hold any planned civil rights demonstrations, but the leaders of the movement decided to go against the ruling and assembled in the centre of the town in readiness for a march to demand equal rights for all citizens of the country. The excitement was palpable. My friends and I felt as if Martin Luther King had just been reborn as a bad-tempered Irishman and was to march around our town with us all in tow. The anticipation was overwhelming for many of us, first time young rebels with the adrenalin flowing and the blood pumping through our veins. Large numbers congregated near the courthouse, a large Victorian building overlooking the town from its vantage at the top of the main street, and very quickly we began to make our noisy presence felt. There were a few speeches from the representatives of the organisers that we could barely hear, and were not even that bothered, and much humour and giggling from the younger members of the audience who seemed to be enjoying the evening's entertainment. It was going to be one of those great memorable nights that we would look back on and wallow in the pleasure of being part of it all. Or so we thought.

It was quickly noted, however, that a gathering of an alternate and aggressive group of protesters was forming at the bottom of the town. With some of these combatants wearing army helmets and carrying pickaxe handles, it quickly became apparent that they were well organised supporters of Ian Paisley, the leader of the Free Presbyterian movement of which Big Ian himself was the founder. It did not look promising, especially as we were told to be like the Mahatma and espouse all violence. The other crowd seemed to have taken a different view and were not averse to a bit of thuggery during their protests. Big Ian's lads were making their presence felt with lots of waving of Union Jacks and the constant singing of *God Save the Queen* and the occasional profanity about the Pope and the Catholic Church.

These demonstrators had obviously been tipped off as to the reason for the gathering of young nationalists outside the town's courthouse and were increasing in size by the minute, whilst all the time being protected by a contingent of well-armed members of the RUC, who faced in our direction and not those of the Free Presbyterian persuasion. It was apparent that there was going to be contact between the two sets of demonstrators. The first move was made by the nationalists who decided to march, 10 and 12 abreast with arms linked as if we were in some black civil rights demonstration in Georgia, down the main street towards the police cordon and the baying crowd of protesters anxiously waiting behind them for the action to begin. Like gladiators in ancient Rome, Big Ian's boys were screaming for blood and the blood of nationalists would certainly add flavour to their evening's entertainment. Meanwhile, my bladder was beginning to fill up and I wasn't altogether sure that I could contain the contents for much longer.

Two police men detain a man after scuffles at the Army barracks in Omagh on Tuesday.

This decision to engage the opposition head on, including their RUC protectors, was not well thought out. As the crowd of nationalists, many young teenagers participating in their first demonstration and thinking it a great big giggle, marched valiantly towards the combatants, the double doors of the courthouse behind us suddenly opened and out poured squads of armed B Specials with police-issue batons in hand whereupon they commenced belting Catholic heads at every opportunity. Those of us who were edging closer to the snarling crowd of Paisley protagonists now stopped in our tracks and seeing what was happening behind, we made a quick about-turn to join the melee at the rear. As we ran back up the hill to support our friends against the sudden, unwelcome introduction from the Specials, the line previously enforced by the RUC suddenly parted like the Dead Sea on a Jewish holiday and gave the crowd an opportunity to pursue us at full pelt. The result was a shit sandwich, some of mine if I am to be totally honest. We were now hemmed in between the proverbial whirling dervishes of the B Specials on one side and the howling hordes of aggrieved Orangemen and members of the RUC on the other.

Ducking, or trying to, the swinging batons from the overweight lumbering constables, we were able to join our comrades without arms in John Street where bottles and bricks were now being launched at the advancing throng of police and Orangemen who, fortuitously, were eventually repulsed. By now the bottles had been filled with a mixture of petrol and paraffin, topped up with soap flakes so that when thrown in the general direction of the police and their accomplices, the flames would be spread by the paraffin and the petrol-infused flaming soap flakes would attach themselves to the tunics of those officers in the front row. The victory was ours even though there were many bloodied heads and countless arrests. Or so we thought.

As we began the task of erecting a makeshift barricade in the middle of John Street, and with great plans to hold our position for as long as we wished, a fusillade of shots rang out from the Lee Enfield rifles held by the Specials, the noise of which sent shudders down our necks and a gush of wee down my pants, the latter brought about through sheer terror. Bullets ricocheting of buildings meant that we were in imminent danger of being accidently shot by the part-time army of farmers who had been instructed to shoot above our heads. Some of these aged marksmen must have forgotten their spectacles as the bullets were whizzing past our heads only a few feet above. The shooting had the desired effect though. It was the first time that many of us had ever been close to the sound of a rifle being fired, and especially in a built-up area the sound was magnified tenfold. We ran.

The following morning, Cassie Ann was eating her boiled egg and looking very stressed.

"What time did you get in last night, my bucko. And do not be lying to your mother because I heard you," she growled between chewing the hard-boiled egg and stirring a cup of tea. I thought that if she had heard me, then why was she asking me about the time I arrived home; but I was not that brave, especially after wetting my pants the night before.

"About two, Mammy, I think," squirming as I answered without meeting her eyes.

"Two, my arse. I heard you creeping up those stairs near five o'clock this morning, you wee shite," her voice now becoming a bit more aggressive. There was just a tiny bit of the egg white hanging from her lower lip which was all that I could focus on.

"And before you start telling me any lies, were you with that crowd wrecking the town during the night? You were seen, so no lying do ye hear me?" she seemed really angry now.

"I was just having a look, Mammy and wasn't really involved that much," I replied. I felt my face going red yet again; that face of mine was my biggest tell-tale sign; can't tell a simple bloody lie but for the face turning bright purple with embarrassment.

"You'll be killed, you know that son, don't you?" she almost whispered her voice seeming to tremble.

"Promise me you won't be getting up to any of that nonsense again. Promise me now in front of that picture of the Blessed Virgin on the mantelpiece," she pleaded. I looked at Cassie Ann and then the Blessed Virgin.

"I promise, Mammy, honestly. No more of that nonsense," I quietly replied. But I could feel the eyes of the Blessed Virgin boring into me as the words came out. That Virgin knew right well that it was not to be the end of my involvement with what was about to happen in that small, troubled part of Ireland.

Turkeys for Christmas

There was a tradition every Christmas for relatives to visit in the days leading up to the celebration of the birth of Christ. Uncles and cousins from the various farms would converge on our house bringing seasonal gifts such as cabbage and sprouts, and of course, a live turkey in a hessian bag tied at the neck to prevent the creature moving too far. The notion was that the turkey would be fresh when killed and after immersion in boiling hot water the skin would be softened thereby easing the plucking of the feathers from its recently deceased carcass. Uncle Francie, a tall, elegant man with oodles of charm, presented the hessian bag to Cassie Ann who expressed her thanks with much gratitude. She enjoyed a fresh turkey. Francie, Felix and my other Uncle Tommy then proceeded to engage in smoking endless *Players* extra-strong untipped cigarettes, flicking the ash in the general direction of the range and chatting about the usual topics, weather and the price of cattle and spuds.

A turkey dinner was a once-a-year event and one that was eagerly anticipated by all the family. The only slight problem was the execution of the turkey. Later that evening, whilst the visitors were still smoking and blethering, Francie suggested that Felix ring the creature's neck. After much toing and froing Felix declined. He would not, could not kill a fly.

"All God's creatures," he would say. Although he would happily eat the turkey.

In the absence of a volunteer, Cassie Ann lifted the hessian bag and extracted a large and not very happy turkey and attempted to put the wriggling creature between her thighs so that she could gain some leverage with the black iron poker in her right hand, the executioner's preferred instrument of death. The turkey fought for its life, but with the assistance of Francie, who held the legs of the by now very agitated bird, Cassie Ann placed the poker under its neck and pulled as hard as she could.

Unfortunately, instead of breaking the turkey's neck, it came off in her left hand. She let out a squeal as she looked at the turkey's head in her hand and promptly screamed as the headless body of the deceased creature instantly flew up towards the ceiling with blood spurting in every direction. Screams from the young ones, pandemonium from the adults and a headless turkey, wings flapping as it flew into walls and chairs, leaving a trail of blood in its wake. Eventually, and it seemed an eternity, the still moving, decapitated Christmas dinner slowed to a few flaps and was captured by a blood-covered Francie. He handed the finally expired creature to Cassie Ann who unceremoniously shoved the bird into a large vat of boiling water and left it to soak before retrieving it and eventually started plucking. It took some time to clean the place of the spilled blood, but for years afterwards the story of the headless turkey spread around the town and was hugely exaggerated. Christmas dinner was special that year. We ate heartily but that was the last time that there was a delivery of a live turkey to our house for Christmas dinner. Her days of decapitating birds in the kitchen with an audience of enthusiastic onlookers was well and truly over.

Felix was a sociable man who enjoyed the company of his many and varied friends. But he and Jim McAleer, with whom he worked for many years delivering pigs and cattle to the abattoir, were inseparable throughout their long lives. Jim and his wife Emily were not natives of the town—Jim coming from a small country village and Emily, with her soft lilting Southern Irish accent, emanating from the Irish Republic. They befriended my parents shortly before both couples were married and remained close friends until the end of their lives. Jim was a frequent visitor at weekends and, accompanied by Felix, they would entertain a small audience gathered in the kitchen with a couple of Irish dances known as 'slides' where only the feet moved in time to the traditional Irish music.

Later in the evening, the assembled crowd of neighbours would play a game of cards called 25, a form of Whist, where passions would run high and gentle arguments would break out if mistakes were made by the partners. Us young ones would gradually be introduced to the game and make the usual mistakes of laying the incorrect cards only to be verbally abused for not paying attention. The game of 25 was popular amongst poor families in the days when the only entertainment was the wireless and there was little of interest to be heard other than where a bomb had exploded and how many were killed or injured.

Cassie Ann enriched those evenings with her passion for the game and for life and would laugh uproariously along with the company of her neighbours and friends. Her face, alive with the joy of being in her own home surrounded by her family, she had finally found peace of mind and with the world. Finally, the smiling, gregarious Cassie Ann had returned to us. Oh, how we had missed that lively gossipy woman. But times were changing in our tiny part of Ireland. And not for the better.

The Christian Brothers

Also known locally as 'Thugs in Cassocks', the Congregation of Christian Brothers was a strict educational institution whose purpose in life was to educate poor children and to provide them with a strong Catholic upbringing. From the age of 5 years up to 17, if a boy was capable enough to pass the 11-plus to qualify for the Grammar School, he would acquire an education at the ever willing but brutal hands of those second-hand priests. In large Catholic families, it was traditional and expected that at least one of the male offspring to study for the priesthood but if there were insufficient funds in the family to pay for the 6 years in the seminary, an acceptable alternative was to join the Christian Brothers at the age of 16 and set out on a life of prayer, educating the poor and enjoying a bit of thuggery thrown in for good measure.

Boys were prepared for passing exams through a combination of relentless study and the remorseless use of the strap, an eight-inch-long leather baton, which was brutally used to thrash young hands, legs and bottoms with all the regularity of the chiming of the Angelus Bell. This precious gift of a free education came with great physical and emotional cost. For many youngsters, the fear of going to school every morning was, at times, overwhelming especially if the first couple of periods were being taught by a neo-psychopathic cleric with a raging hangover. Who really cared how long it took three men, digging a hole 10 yards deep and 50 feet long with two shovels and a pick? An earth digger was not the answer and a thump across the face for being insolent was the response.

The original good intentions of the organisation, founded by Edmund Rice—a wealthy individual from Waterford, were to ensure that children, especially those from a poor background, received a religious education. Over the years, the Christian Brothers, who were required to take vows of chastity, poverty and obedience, but somehow managed to miss out on a vow of abstinence from alcohol, developed a reputation as violent educators who would not think twice about beating the living daylights out of their young charges. Complaining to one's parents was unheard of as the only alternate to an education for a poor Catholic lad in the town was the local Protestant school and what decent, Mass-going parent would want that sort of schooling for her beloved children.

Brother Doyle, a man with the facial appearance of a constipated weasel and one leg shorter that the other, was known throughout the school and beyond, as Hop Doyle. An unhappy little creature with a penchant for occasional bouts of thuggery, he managed large classrooms of poorly dressed scrawny youngsters with great efficiency that was ably supported with frequent use of the thick leather strap that he would brutally use on the hands and on the backs of the bare legs of his young charges. This combination of fear and violence worked well as many children were capable, at the very least, of reading and writing from a relatively early age. Hop Doyle was an outwardly pious little excuse for a man. He was always seen at Mass at the Sacred Heart Church and at the Rosary that was said each evening during the so-called holy months of May and October. Seated in or near the front pew, he attended every funeral of any prominent local who had had enough of life and he made absolutely certain that he was present at their wakes to express his sympathy with the expectation of a few glasses of whiskey and a donation to the church by way of recompense for his prayers for the bereaved.

The school was a stickler for cleanliness. Twice yearly, the District Nurse would visit to conduct a thorough inspection of the heads of the youngsters for lice, sometimes referred to as nits. These little parasites are found on human heads and feed on blood on the scalp and are usually on those skulls of children that had not seen soap, never mind shampoo, in quite a long time.

Head lice is spread from person to person through direct contact with the hair of an infected person, of which there were many in that school of unwashed youngsters. The nurse would check each cranium for the tiny white specks and, when found, she would use a sharp metal comb to scrape the creatures from the infected head usually at the cost of much bleeding and lots of crying from the pupils. During the hair inspection of each child, Hop Doyle would be in close attendance and would tut each time a child was found to be infected, usually to the annoyance of the unfortunate nurse who was desperately trying to work her way through so many young heads. Hop did not have to worry about catching head lice as he was as bald as a Parson's Nose. A note from the nurse would be handed to the pupil who was identified with severe head lice to be given to his mother to seek suitable treatment. We were always recipients of such notes. Cassie Ann's home remedy would be to scrub our heads with carbolic soap and then viciously use her very own short-tooth lice comb to such effect that our heads would bear the marks for many days.

Hop Doyle was a sour little man with a big appetite for beating the living daylights out of little boys, but worse was to come. Much worse.

Cassie Ann was keen that I should attend the Grammar School. However, there were several hurdles for her to overcome. Getting me into the class that sat the 11-plus examination entailed her dragging her ten-year-old scruffily dressed boy up to the Parochial House for a confrontation with the Parish Priest. After a prolonged period of her berating the unfortunate cleric about the failure of the Catholic Church to cater for the poorest of the poor in the community, he finally relented. Fear rather than compassion swayed his decision. The Parish Priest was not a man for arguments and entering into one with a combative Cassie Ann was not one that he could win. That following September along with 38 other frightened weans, I arrived at the entrance to the temporary school known as '*the Huts*' located near the local Gaelic football pitch, a few hundred yards from our house in Brook Street. For the youngsters given an opportunity to gain entry to the Grammar School, our classroom was in a prefabricated hut that was split into two sections, one for the boys taking the 11-plus exam and the other room for those educationally less fortunate. Both rooms were heated by a coal-burning stove that was replenished during the day depending upon the weather conditions outside. It was to be a very long year for us all.

Brother Ennis, also known as the Menace and our teacher and religious instructor for the many long weeks and months ahead, was a very athletic and well-built twenty something from some distant county in the far South of Ireland. Initially, to us aspiring Grammar school boys, his sole purpose in life was one of inflicting as much pain on children as possible. With a hint of madness in his eyes, he relished the role of teacher cum punisher. The fear of walking into the classroom on that first day was palpable. We had heard rumours of his brutality, and now here we all were looking at that imposing specimen of a thug as he stood at the front of the assembled class—his black cassock neatly ironed, his ecumenical collar gleaming white and holding a long, thick black strap gripped in his large right hand. He meant business, but of what we had no real idea. In an accent that we barely understood, he conveyed to us that his calling, as a man of God, was to ensure that as many as possible of his pupils would walk proudly through the gates of the Grammar school the following September, and if it took violence to achieve this aim, then so be it. It was not very long before the thuggery and the beatings commenced.

The following Monday morning, we all lined up for the results of the previous week's English test. I was particularly nervous as Cassie Ann had been unwell and had taken to the bed again which resulted in us having to fend for ourselves and, in turn, that meant that my homework was less than satisfactory. When I offered my right hand for the obligatory punishment from his leather strap, he noticed that both the hand and wrist were filthy. He proceeded to check my left hand, then the back of my neck, all of which were unwashed and '*disgusting*' as he loudly announced to the other 38 boys. After some histrionics and an outpouring of contempt from the cleric and my pleading that my mother was not very well, he directed me to the lavatory at the far end of the adjoining classroom. As I walked through the other classroom towards the cubicle, in a raised voice I could hear him proclaim to the lay teacher in charge of those less fortunate in his class, that a dirty boy was on his way to wash himself, something that he should have attended to before making his appearance at school. A mixture of pity and fear was etched upon their faces, as with my head down, I scurried towards the lavatory and scrubbed every visible part of my body with as much vigour as I could muster and with the help of a large bar of red carbolic soap.

When I retraced my steps to the classroom, Brother Ennis was busy doling out punishment to many of my compatriots for their failures in the proscribed homework. In between the lashings, he clocked me through the corner of his eye and promptly halted the beatings. With a grin on his face, he instructed me to hold out my right hand for inspection followed by six lashes from a great height with the leather strap in his hefty right hand. He then inspected the left hand and when satisfied, he kindly provided me with another six lashes. The hands may have been clean but after the punishment they stung to the point of near numbness. Shortly afterwards we stood for prayers and broke for lunch. The goodness and mercy of Our Lord was bestowed upon us once again. But I did not cry during the beatings, nor afterwards. Nearly, but I would not give him the pleasure of seeing tears drain from my frightened eyes.

Thereafter, even in the coldest mornings I would scrub my hands and neck assiduously in the job box outside the back door of our house in Brook Street. As for the beatings I never dared mention them to Cassie Ann. She was not well so it was best to leave her alone so that she could recover. She had her own worries and demons to conquer without having to worry about me and my sore hands.

On the first Friday of every month, Ennis the Menace would announce to his captive audience that contributions for the poor black babies in Africa would be collected the following Monday and we were required to ask our parents for any spare money so that the unfortunate babies could be helped. This was known as 'A Penny for the Black Babies' charity but for all we knew not a penny ever went anywhere near a black baby or a baby of any other colour for that matter. We had no money in our house, never mind spare money. When I could pluck up the courage to ask Cassie Ann for any spare money that she didn't have, she would look at me for a few seconds and put her hand to her mouth and say a quiet Hail Mary. But every Monday morning, without fail, she would put some money in the little black baby envelope and I would deliver it into the hands of Ennis the Menace. He never expressed his thanks, ever. He would just snatch the envelope containing the money and put it with all the other envelopes into a large tin box beside his leather strap—both resting on his desk at the front of the classroom. We were never altogether sure if the black babies in Africa ever saw the spare money that Cassie Ann and other mothers had unwillingly contributed but we hoped that they might have seen some.

Ennis the Menace enjoyed playing the Irish national sports of Gaelic football and Hurling. He was from a part of Ireland where only these two sports were played and games such as hockey and soccer were forbidden. He sought to instil in his pupils that same love for the games that was ingrained in him from an early age and when it came to Gaelic football, a game where the ball is kicked or passed hand-to-hand, he was assiduous in ensuring that we all knew the rules and strictly adhered to them. One bright sunny afternoon, when he was refereeing a game of Gaelic football, a talented little lad who had a penchant for playing soccer, deliberately dribbled the football with his right foot and dazzled a few of the defenders with some really neat turns and deft touches and eventually scored a smartly taken goal. We clapped his efforts as we were all fans of either Danny Blanchflower of Tottenham Hotspur fame or Harry Greig from Manchester United but Ennis the Menace went ballistic. He hated that alien game with a fierce passion. Unbeknownst to the lad Ennis ran at full pelt after the smiling little soccer player who, upon seeing what was coming, suddenly stopped in his tracks. With a look of sheer horror on his wretched face, the raging bull of a man galloped towards him and grabbed the boy around the neck.

"We don't play that foreign game here, you filthy little brat," screamed Ennis his spittle spraying over the face of the petrified lad.

"You will play Gaelic as it is meant to be played, or you will know all about it," continued the teacher as he laid into the lad with the back of both hands leaving the boy in a crying heap on the turf.

"Get up and stop your snivelling, you ridiculous boy and leave this pitch immediately," he shouted down at the boy whose face was now streaming with tears.

We continued to play his form of Gaelic football until the end of the school year but no one was foolhardy enough to dribble a ball thereafter even if it was the most sensible approach at times.

Through good fortune rather than any small measurement of brainpower, I managed to somehow succeed in the 11-plus exam. We left behind the thug who helped us to achieve his aim of achieving his goal of ensuring so many of us qualified to attend the big school where even more Thugs in Cassocks were waiting to batter the living daylights out of us. We were not sad to see the back of Ennis the Menace. Now it was a case of seven more years in the unyielding environment of force-fed Catholicism, unrelenting violence from clerics and lay teachers and a lifelong detestation of anything wearing a black cassock.

By the time the results of the 11-plus were announced, Cassie Ann had recovered sufficiently to loudly inform all the neighbours in Brook Street that her second youngest, the spotty one, was about to join the elite at the Grammar School in early September. It was not so much a boast, rather it was a small relief that something good had happened at long last and she had to express her feelings in the best way she knew. Tilly (short for Matilda) Noble, who helped me with my homework on occasions, was delighted for my success and promptly rewarded me with some money and a kiss on the cheek, my first ever embrace from the opposite sex. Tilly had her false teeth in place for the occasion.

There was a downside, though. Cassie Ann was unable to afford the new uniform. Not only the requirement to be kitted out in the school blazer, blue shirts, grey shorts, the regulation tie and, of course, black shoes and grey socks. There were also many books that had to be bought or acquired, a list of which were kindly provided by the *Brothers*, the nickname that we would use when referring to the school. Historically, there was a commercial arrangement between all the Catholic schools and a clothing shop on the main street of the town whereby all uniforms had to be bought in that emporium. As it happened, the uniforms were not for sale in any other establishment so it was a case of either buy from the appointed retailer and ensure that the Catholic Church received a kickback or simply do not turn up on the first day of school. Cassie Ann, however, was a resourceful woman. A second-hand store of sorts that sold a myriad of clothing and shoes was open six days a week in the back market just off Bridge Street where all sorts of used blazers and trousers could be had at a knock down price. The shop was run by a man called McGovern, who according to my mother,

"Knew the price of everything and the value of nothing," as she would frequently say to her neighbours after picking up a few bargains from McGovern. It was there that she found for me a blazer with the school badge which, when I tried it on, was noticeably far too big for me. But the blazer looked almost new with just a fee bare patches on the elbows but not a problem as it was going cheap and was to be mine for the foreseeable future. McGovern also had a varied selection of black lace-up shoes for boys of my age and my mother eventually agreed a price for the blazer and the two mismatched shoes and then off we went in search of a pair of the mandatory short grey trousers. These she acquired in a St Vincent de Paul shop in George's Street and although they looked like new and presentable, nevertheless, they were far too big for me and came down way past my knees. Her response when I queried the size was to inform me, quite forcibly, that I would grow into them and to hold my tongue.

She was right, of course. Within a couple of years, the trousers looked the part as I quickly grew taller, put on some weight, and although carrying a noticeable number of patches on the rear end due to wear and tear, the inspecting Brothers never twigged that I was wearing hand-me-downs. Or they did know and took pity on me and turned the proverbial blind eye. Would have been a first though.

After a long, sweltering summer, the day finally arrived for me to make my appearance at the Christian Brothers Grammar School. Cassie Ann looked me up and down in the kitchen, spat on her hand with which she tried to smooth down some unruly hairs on my head and checked that I was presentable. She had left a single-room country school at the age of 11 with barely enough education to allow her to read and write. She had missed so many schooldays slaving for her stepfather on their tiny few acres in the back end of Donegal, and since life was cruel in that remote part of Ireland, the notion of mandatory education was not a requirement. You were taught the basics and off back to the farm you went and to the milking of the cows. Now she had a son about to embark on a Grammar School education from a house at the far end of Brook Street.

"Look at you. Would you just look at my wean and him going to that posh school? They will be jealous of you cub but don't you worry and just make me proud. And stay away from those Protestant girls do you hear me? We want none

86

of that nonsense around this house." she said directly to my face but with an enormous grin that stretched from ear to ear. She then put on her overcoat, her only overcoat and the one that was used both in winter and during the summer months and announced to the rest if the family that it was her intention to walk me down to the end of Brook Street so that the neighbours could have a good look at her son going to the big school. On that balmy September morning, Cassie Ann marched beside her trembling son wearing his second-hand uniform down that little street and waved at any neighbouring woman who was hanging over their half door and proclaimed in great voice,

"My wean is going to the Christian Brothers, did you know that!" By the second shout at another unfortunate onlooker, I could feel my face turning deep purple with embarrassment. "That's my cub in his brand-new uniform," she continued whilst throwing me a wink. Eventually, we arrived at the end of the street and she turned towards me and looked into my eyes, "Make me proud son, that's a good boy." With that she turned around and quickly walked back towards the hovel that we called home. The way that she strode out with her handbag swinging back and forth in her right hand I could tell that she had a big grin on her face, the cat that got the milk grin.

The Grammar school was located up a narrow lane just off Castle Street, directly opposite Gormley's Pub, my father and uncle's favourite watering hole. Walking into the school yard I could see a collection of drab-looking prefabs adjacent to the main building and only a stone's throw from the Parochial House to the right and to the left the walled garden belonging to the Church of Ireland Vicar. Trapped between two warring religions in effect. Those of us from the 11-plus class met at the bottom of the slight incline that led to the school's tarred playground and looked to each other for mutual support. Each of us appeared as hesitant as the next because we knew that for many years hence, life was never going to be easy. Here we all were at the commencement of the first term in the 'big' school as we lined up one after another on the playground to be greeted by the Principal of the school, a sinister looking individual whom we knew as Brother Herbert whose nickname behind his back was 'Herbie'. He was a tall, fearsome looking man with a long, gaunt neck that reminded me of a wading bird, a heron in a slow-moving river. He had a shock of greased-back white hair and long bony hands that menacingly, and very slowly, waved a long, thick black leather strap back and forth across his dandruff-covered cassock for us all to see. And to fear. He spoke quietly, so much so that we had to lean forward to catch every measured word that came out of his narrow lips. Ireland's version of Count Dracula had materialised right in front of us. Bram Stoker would have been right at home in such a setting.

'Study hard, adhere to the Holy Commandments and pass your exams' was the summation of his address to the fearful audience. And do not step out of line as you will feel the wrath of His temper and this strap will be His messenger. There was no doubting his sincerity about the use of the strap. As he spoke in those hushed tones, I could feel a trickle of pee running down my second-hand short trousers. I did not dare look or even touch my damp pants, though. Jesus, that Herbie was some scary man. A man of God sent to scare the living daylights out of us. To be avoided at all costs was my immediate thought.

Each school day commenced with a litany of prayers followed by the teaching of a multiplicity of subjects that were frequently interspersed with bouts of varying degrees of violence. Books, well used ones, had to be purchased— putting even more financial strain on Cassie Ann. The subjects ranged from Latin and Irish through to the usual mathematics and history and, of course, religious education or more commonly known as Catholic indoctrination. The teaching of Catholicism was mandatory of course. Every day, at every opportunity, we prayed. Mornings began with prayers. Afternoons began with more prayers, more thuggish teaching and ranting from the teachers and home-time concluded with prayers before home time. Boys very quickly were transformed from smiling children to young men whose faces were etched with constant fear and trepidation. Thuggery, but fortunately no buggery, was what lay in store for us all for the foreseeable future.

The first four years passed slowly. It was more like a prison sentence with hard labour than simply receiving an education. Then unexpectedly came the announcement that we were moving to a brand spanking, figuratively speaking, new school on the Kevlin Road, about half a mile from our present location. The Catholic Church, with a begrudging contribution from the Unionist Government, dipped deep into its many financial pockets and a new school with all the latest technology was made available to us. We fortunate pupils, half boys and half men with tiny pockets of hair sprouting from our acned faces and other parts of the nether region, would be the first of the new entrants to cross the gates of that resplendent new place of learning for Catholic boys from far and wide. And so it came to pass. The following September we moved into our pristine new halls of learning and sure enough the place was impressive with a gym and even the indoor toilets looked as if you could enjoy a good shite in them without catching frostbite of the bum. The school was located close to the centre of the town which was a bonus except that we were not permitted to leave the premises during the school day. Still, we could slowly wander home after school and ogle at the fine-looking female talent from the nearby Protestant Academy providing of course that none of their male counterparts were lurking nearby. There was always something about those young ladies from that other faith that signalled a certain allure about them the tight-fitting uniforms with short skirts. Lust was a dreadful feeling but we wallowed in it nonetheless.

A few hundred yards from our seat of learning was that very Academy. The major difference between the two establishments was that the Protestant boys and girls were educated in mixed classrooms with them seated beside each other unlike us unfortunate Catholics who had to contend with all-male environments where we were high on testosterone but short on any sexual action. A small group of friends used to meet after school most days to discuss, at great length, which of the Academy girls was the best looking and approachable. Our imaginations would run wild at the thought of having to sit beside a girl all day long without trying to comprehend some daft bit of Latin prose taught by a man in a cassock covered in dandruff. The other key difference was that the Protestant girls looked so smart and tidy compared to the girls in the nearby Catholic Loreto Convent. The latter were required to wear dull brown blazers with a bright yellow trim and extra-long skirts to hide any white flesh that might entice us boys into thinking bad thoughts. On the other hand, the Academy wore pristine blue blazers and skirts so short that us spotty-faced young men had great difficulty in containing our lustful aspirations for the fulfilment of our sexual desires. We would have given anything just to be an Academy boy for a day. But the ever-watchful Christian Brothers were extremely aware of these lustful desires lurking in the minds and bodies of their charges. Prayers, more prayers, morning Mass and weekly attendance at confession was their remedy for such behaviour. It did not work.

There was one cassock-cloaked cleric who was as close to being a psychopath as one could ever meet. Red-faced with a drinker's nose and a violent, unpredictable temper coupled with what seemed like a perverse pleasure in dispensing harsh punishment to young men if he thought that they transgressed any of his rules, never mind those of the Church. Brutality was the norm in that institution. Their reputation for inflicting beatings on lads who had transgressed the rules were known through the county. The fear of brutal punishment from some thuggish cleric always took precedence over the desire to learn. On occasions everything would be calm with heads bent forward studying some obscure Irish poet and then, without warning, the rage of the psychopath would suddenly erupt for whatever trivial reason and the nearest boy would be viciously thumped on the back of the head. On one occasion, his face purple with inner rage, he took hold of the wooden duster used for cleaning the blackboard in his right hand and when a timid young lad was unable to answer a question in Irish sufficiently quick enough, he split open the boy's skull with the duster resulting in blood running down the unfortunate boy's neck. A bright and highly intelligent lad who had a stammer, he was taken from the classroom to have the blood stemmed and to be patched up in readiness for another clobbering. We never saw him again.

However, there were periods of levity amidst all this thuggery. A lay teacher, who endeavoured to teach French to boys whose command of the English language was a struggle at the best of times, often felt the need to take the strap to those whom he considered were not making sufficient effort to pronounce certain words in his preferred subject. His nickname was Gaucho, named after the cowboys in Argentina. Where this moniker originated from no one ever discovered but Gaucho seemed somehow appropriate for the man. His eyebrows were his most prominent feature, unusually thick and angry, and constantly undulating above his blood-stained, rheumy eyes. It was if they were small ferrets furrowing into his forehead. Frank, his real name, was a sad and lonely man who was nearing the end of his teaching days and where once he was feared sadly he was now treated with derision as a foolish old man with his best days far behind him. Life for Gaucho was not pleasant. The unfortunate man never married and his only meaningful relationship was with a bottle of whiskey that he consumed every evening in a rundown hotel in the town accompanied by smoking endless untipped Gallaghers Blues cigarettes. He was a native of County Cork in the far south of the country and for many years he lived in the local hostelry at a heavily discounted rate and spent his evenings and weekends drinking, smoking and reading.

If he had an early morning class, he would spend the first ten minutes gazing out of the open window and coughing his lungs up whilst trying to catch his breath even in winter. The cigarettes had taken their toll over the years and here he was, barely able to function, standing in front of an unruly class who knew that they could take advantage of him in his sad, final years of his chosen profession. On one occasion, he attempted to instil some discipline into the boys, all around 15 or 16 years of age, by attempting to use the thick leather belt provided by the school. It was not a success. He lined up everyone and commenced slapping the hands of each boy with the strap. But his power was no longer there, nor was his stamina. By the time he had finished the first batch, we lined up again to take further punishment and it was only after he recognised one of the boys holding his hands out for seconds that he gave up, sat down breathless and never uttered another word for the remainder of the period.

A few years later, I bumped into Gaucho in the town and took him for a drink or three. We had a long chat and after a few large whiskies, he related the story of his life that afternoon in Bogan's Bar. His time on this earth had not been a happy one. He had studied at Trinity College Dublin and was awarded a First in French after which he lived in Normandy for a spell. It was there where he met the love of his life, 'a stunningly beautiful woman', he reminisced as he stared into the glass of whisky. "French, sophisticated and truly stunning. I knew from the outset that she far too good for me but I prayed a lot," he stared across the table at me with his bloodshot eyes and his thin, skeletal hands trembling. For a few minutes, he looked almost wistful as he thought back on that memory of his lost love. He explained that he had tried to persuade her to return with him to a very backward and cold, unwelcoming Ireland but she refused instead preferring the comfort and freedom of France. "And who could blame her," he whispered in between a bout of coughing and retching.

"Why didn't you stay in France with her?" I asked.

"I was homesick. May God forgive me," he replied. "For Cork of all bloody places," said Gaucho.

After the rejection of his one true love, the life of Gaucho McLaughlin gradually ebbed away over his remaining years. He had been a superb rugby player during his days at Trinity College in Dublin and was quite an athlete, he loved the Arts and enjoyed the company of literary types. And now, for reasons that he would not elaborate upon, he was stuck in a job that he hated and in a town that was alien to him and his life quietly drifting by in a sea of drink and a fog of cigarettes. Frank McLaughlin eventually died in a pub owned by his brother in his native Cork City. A wasted life.

In Pursuit of the Opposite Sex

As sixteen-year-old, we were required to sit in silence for a 30-minute lesson on the much-anticipated subject of sex. Sex, girls, snogging were subjects that were always uppermost in our minds most days. We were spotty-faced horny young sixteen-year-old virgins who just wanted to experience the simple pleasure of the close company of a girl for a few hours or so. It did not really matter what the girl looked like, fat or thin, tall or small, as long as she was a female that would suffice. That afternoon the Christian Brother, the one tasked with enlightening us about all things relating to sexuality and the workings of the female body, was the much-feared, nicotine-smelling, always hungover Headmaster, a man who would not tolerate any interruptions during his lecture on all things sexual. This was to be a major disappointment. So many questions on so many topics, such as the big one, intimacy with females, any females, and what was a lad supposed to do, should the occasion ever arise, about fiddling with her bits up above never mind the down below bits. Would Hell beckon if French kissing ever occurred and was it a mortal sin to constantly have naughty thoughts about what girls wore under their kimonos? These and many more questions had been discussed and argued over by an informal committee of acne-scarred young men before finally compiling the definitive list with which to quiz the appointed instructor who would answer all our questions, or so we hoped.

There he was. The mad 48-year-old virgin Headmaster, standing in front of the class of sex-hungry lads with their extensive list of questions. All of us were desperate to find out so much about so many things of which we knew so little. Mr Scary, the Head Honcho Christian Brother, who would frighten Vlad the Impaler, was the man who was supposed to lead us into a world of sexual enlightenment after which we would know what to do with girls and how often, hopefully. After he made the Sign of the Cross which, of course, required us to do the same, he glared at us all and very slowly looked around the room. In a thick Southern Irish accent, he finally pronounced, "I will not be taking any questions from you lot, so sit back and learn. Do you hear me?"

"Yes, Brother," we chanted in unison. My cousin Norby, who pretended that he knew more about the female anatomy than the rest of us put together, was seen scratching his testicles out of boredom.

We sat back for 30 minutes and listened. We learned sweet nothing. Not a word about snogging. Not even a word about when we could even consider fiddling with the naughty bits that girls had and we desired. And not even a mention about when tongues could be employed which was one of the many questions my friend, John the Landlord (his father owned a bit of land out in the country hence the nickname), was going to ask but never had the opportunity. We were as one in believing that boys putting their tongues in girls' mouths and vice versa, was considered as important and exciting as the fondling of the upper bits of girls. I had never experienced such titillation but the cousin claimed that he had performed such activity on numerous occasions with many girls and that it was very desirable indeed. Sitting in that classroom, listening to that cleric talking about 'dis and dat' because he could not pronounce 'this and that', was the most enormous anti-climax. Not that many of us actually knew what a decent climax was.

The Mad Christian Brother, who never once mentioned the word 'sex', not even once, however did leave us with one memorable, final piece of advice.

"Don't be touching yourselves down there," as he half-gestured towards the crutch of his trousers whilst standing in front of the class.

"You will go straight to Hell if you do," said he as his face grew even more red. He shouted the words in the general direction of the open-mouthed audience at the top of his voice. Mind you I was convinced that he was looking directly at Cousin Norby whom he hated with an almighty passion. Norby's dad owned a local taxi firm, but he was also skilled at manufacturing the thick black-leather belts with which the teachers were allocated to beat the pupils at regular intervals. As much as the Christian Brother would have enjoyed giving my cousin a regular beating, the consequences would have been no more new straps. With those final words of defiance, the Sex Meister made a quick Sign of the Cross and without waiting to see if we had followed his example, he turned sharply on the heels of his shoes and made to leave the room. Unfortunately, for him, his cassock caught in the door as he closed it thus requiring him to re-open the door in order to extract the rest of the garment. Eyes glaring and his face a beetroot red he banged the door shut behind him, having made sure all his clothing had safely exited the classroom.

My cousin Norby's response was to stand up in front of the class, grab his groin and utter just one word 'Cock'. That once frightened and deeply disappointed group of horny young men now collapsed into fits of long overdue hysterical laughter. But nevertheless, it still remained that we were in desperate need of answers to so many vital questions. These questions, and many more, had to be answered before we could get a good night's sleep ever again.

That evening, seriously pissed off about the complete failure to find enlightenment about the mystery and pleasures of the female body and our own sexuality, a few of us met in the town's only decent coffee shop and agreed on a plan of action whereby we would seek answers to our ever-increasing list of important sex questions. The town library. But, of course, there must be myriad books in that depository at the far end of the town where we could glean all the information that we required but had been denied to us by the virgin cleric. Our plan was to visit the library in small groups of two certainly no more than three so as not to raise any suspicion, on a mission of enlightenment and when armed with the relevant knowledge we would share our findings with the full group afterwards. When the surreptitious visit to the library was finally executed, we congregated in our kitchen one Friday evening when Cassie Ann was at Bingo and Felix was having a drink in Gormley's with his brothers. Sadly, our efforts were not well rewarded. The net result was that we had obtained several pages torn from a number of anatomical and medical books showing drawings of the female torso. But no actual pictures. No naughty bits of what girls are supposed to look like down below, the important bits, and not even a good picture of the top parts either although the cousin had insisted that he was quite familiar with that part of the female anatomy already and was insistent on explaining the details to anyone who would listen. All we had for our combined efforts after that daring trip to the town library was a couple of black and white images and a few diagrams of the female body with arrows pointing to bits that made no sense and were about as stimulating as a wet Irish Bank Holiday Monday in May.

County Cinema

There were two cinemas in the town. The larger of the two and the most popular was called the County Cinema and hosted all the major films over many generations. The County, as it was known, was located in the centre of the town and was very handy for a few drinks in the nearby local pubs either before the evening performance of just after the end and, of course the obligatory rendition of God Save the Queen to remind those attending just who was the real government of that little part of the UK that nestled in the North West of the island of Ireland.

Cassie Ann's one and only venture to the cinema, or pictures as she referred to the place, was with Felix to see a black and white film directed by Alfred Hitchcock that frightened her so much that she never returned to the cinema again. She had no reservations in her children enjoying seeing films and would always ask about what we had seen but nothing would ever tempt her to return to the place. For the penniless youngsters of the town, Saturday mornings were the highlight of the week. Free from the brutality and indoctrination by the clerics, we would descend on the cinema building for the 10 am matinee showing of some cowboy and western film, or space movie, and rush past the few attendants at the doors as soon as they were opened without paying the admission. They had no desire to chase after a group of noisy, unwashed nine-year-olds, so for the sake of their sanity, they just allowed the majority of us to pass them by and grab a seat where we could. Sitting as close to the front as possible, the excited weans would scream in anticipation as soon as the lights dimmed and the heavy red velvet curtains slowly drew back. The yelling from the overexcited youngsters would reach fever pitch and within seconds, they would be mesmerised by the action on the screen in front of them. Between the Lone Ranger, Roy Rogers and Buck Rogers, it was a toss-up to see who received the most cheers when they appeared on the big screen. A tanner to get in, if you had to cough up provided the opportunity to scream at good old Flash Gordon and Ming the Merciless striving to always outdo each other, to enjoy the numerous cowboy heroes such as the legendry Hop Along Cassidy and Billy the Kid. The good guys always wore the white ten-gallon hats and clean shirts with tassels whilst the baddies wore all black outfits not unlike the Christian Brothers.

The main feature was usually Roy Rodgers on his trusty steed or Tarzan, a white man wearing only a loincloth running around a make-believe Hollywood jungle with a monkey as his partner whilst antagonising the local black population. The indomitable king of the jungle would holler or yell for animals to come to the rescue of some lost maiden and this would be echoed by all the youngsters in the cinema. For an hour or so we were all of us aspiring Tarzans.

"A fiery horse with the speed of light, a cloud of dust and a hearty Hi-Yo Silver—The Lone Ranger." He was the real hero of our youth along with his trusty Native American sidekick, Tonto, who referred to his boss as Kemo Sabbe, a term of endearment. After the end of the matinee, children would run amok amongst the crowds of weekly shoppers pretending to be Red Indians with their hands over the mouths, emulating an Apache war cry or pointing their forefingers in a pistol-like fashion pretending to shoot each other and falling down pretend dead on the footpath in front of the butchers' shop. Hordes of screaming children would run for home slapping the backsides (sorry, horses) whilst avoiding any ambush on the way. "I'm Tonto, no, I'm Tonto, you can be Kemo Sabbe," would be the call from the posse of excited howling youngsters. Old ladies out shopping would tut and grumble and rattle their false teeth at such noisy behaviour, but it was too much fun not to run wild across the prairies being chased by murdering Red Indians in short trousers and snotty noses after a Saturday morning matinee show at the Pictures in that little Irish country town. "'Hi Yo, Silver! Away!"

For teenagers, the County Cinema was also a place to meet on an early Saturday evening to watch films such as: The Invisible Man, who was always visible but wrapped in crepe bandages from head to toe and who could solve nigh impossible mysteries and miraculously defy the bad guys who were trying to expose him. When the crepe bandages were removed, his invisible being would evade all capture and he would right whatever wrong that was required and then miraculously re-appear without a bandage out of place. There was one film that captured all our imaginations as teenagers. It was the 1966 Italian epic Spaghetti Western film directed by Sergio Leone and starring Clint Eastwood as 'the Good', Lee Van Cleef as 'the Bad' and Eli Wallach as 'the Ugly' with a memorable score by Enrico Morricone, the Italian composer. The plot revolved around three opposing gunslingers competing with each other to find a vast fortune in a buried cache of Confederate gold amidst the violent chaos of the American Civil War. The audience would sit in hushed anticipation and wallow in the suspense as the film reached its climax. The film had the protagonists located in a deserted graveyard with Leone's slow, long shots focussing on each of their faces and the words quietly spoken by Eastwood to Lee Van Cleef

"You see, in this world, there's two kinds of people, my friend. Those with loaded guns and those who dig. You dig." Oh, how we memorised those words and would drop them into conversations for many years afterwards.

As the final duel ensued, Clint walks away with his share of the gold having despatched Van Cleef with a shot to the chest whilst leaving Wallach alive but tied up lying on top of his share of the gold in the grave that he had been forced to dig. Sitting in that cinema with friends enjoying watching our heroes such as John Wayne, Steve McQueen and Clint transporting us to never, never land and places we could only ever dream of made that made life bearable. At the time the only violence was on the screen and not on the streets outside. That would soon change.

Girls

They were everywhere. Catholic girls in brown jackets with garish yellow trim jackets, long hair covering spotty faces, wearing extra-long skirts to hide their much valued and well-protected virginity. Protestant girls in smart blue blazers with short dark blue skirts, just above the knee. Girls with big front lumps under their tight blue jumpers and girls with nothing up top. Girls with long legs, girls with fat bums and girls with no bums. There was no shortage of girls. They were everywhere and yet we could not get within touching distance of any of them. Not even the remotest chance of a quick snog at the rear of the bus depot after the schools were finished for the day and the country girls having to travel back to their families on the farms.

My pals and I would hang around the bus depot late afternoons and early evenings whether it was raining or not, a regular occurrence in that wet part of our Irish world, and gaze with unbridled envy at the Protestant boys who would accompany the smartly dressed girls on to the buses. We would stare at them as they sat together in the back seats and, occasionally, they would give a slight wave to us lustful virgins as the bus departed. We so wanted to be a Protestant lad for a day or two. Please God, just a few days and we promise to be really good when we return to the faith. And miss Confession for a week or two just to be on the safe side.

Social gatherings for local youths from both communities were as rare as finding hen's teeth. Catholics had their celli evenings where there was dancing to Irish traditional music; not exactly conducive to getting off with the opposite sex especially when it was a set dance such as the Siege of Ennis where partners try their best to violently swing each other around the hall whilst pretending that we were enjoying ourselves. Especially, the larger, more muscular girls from the rural communities who rejoiced in such dancing and didn't bother too much about romance. The Protestant young ones had their very own discos with modern music from the charts. These took place in the local Orange Hall, or in the Scout and Guide Hut, with improvised DJs and endless smooching to slow songs. We had heard so much about these dances and discos but were too frightened to try to gain entry. Catholics could not participate in either organisation but on one late dark autumn Saturday evening, we heard about a session that was happening in the Orange Hall on Sedan Avenue. We decided to gate-crash the bash especially as we now had made friends with a couple of lads from the 'other side' who promised that they would help us break the ice, or our jaws if it all went tits up. Accompanied by Tall Tom, the Protestant son of the Manager of the town's Post Office, we paid our entrance fee and with a degree of nonchalance, we wandered around the packed hall nodding to groups of girls who were looking at us as if we had just arrived from a seminary in Rome. There were a few raised eyebrows from some of the Protestant lads but there was no animosity or antagonism but merely a nod of recognition here and there and then on with the dancing. Surprisingly, and with no little envy on my part, several of my colleagues had some success with several girls including that lecherous cousin of mine who disappeared for an hour and when returned he had a stupid look on his smug face.

There were to be many more evenings when we would venture into those Protestant discos and desperately try to chat-up the good looking and well-scrubbed girls. At long last life seemed worth living in that divided little town. But the pleasure of those Saturday evenings was to end abruptly. At the Monday morning school assembly, Vlad the headmaster, his face so red that we thought that he was about to self-combust, stood in the middle of the stage, flanked by his staff, some with visible hangovers and glared at the captive audience. We could sense that serious trouble was brewing.

"News has reached my ears that some of you boys have been seen in Protestant dancing establishments at weekends. I will not ask those who are guilty of these wilful sins against our precious religion to raise your filthy hands but I know who you all are. This is your one and final warning. If I hear of any of that disgraceful behaviour in the future, you will have me to deal with," he growled as he produced his long leather strap from the deep pocket of his cassock and waved it high in the air. Shite, we had been rumbled. Those of us who were guilty tried not to look at each other for fear of some eagle-eyed clerical thug catching sight of our worried faces. Instead, we waited until the morning break and huddled together behind the handball alley at the area of the school, the same handball alley where older lads would have a quick cigarette. It was concluded that some nosey mother had heard, or had got wind of our nocturnal excursions, and had warned the clergy of the impending damage to our precious souls if this nonsense was not terminated with immediate effect. We made a collective decision to take a break from our sojourns with those beguiling girls from the other side of town and start attending the dances for Catholics only again. There was one fine-looking, well-endowed girl by the name of Hazel whom I had met a few times at those dances, though, to be honest, she barely ever looked at me.

Just thought she was merely toying with me and sadly it all ended before the romance had a chance to blossom. All that endless lovely lusting over lovely Protestant girls was now over. Thanks to some nosey old cow of a mother.

There were the occasional dances in the Foresters Hall for older teenagers. The establishment was owned by an institution called the Irish National Foresters who were categorised as a friendly society that just happened to support Irish Nationalism and had over a quarter of a million members in 1,000 branches worldwide. But in our town, it was a meeting place for the locals to play Bingo every Friday or Saturday evening, where there were the occasional dances for the young and old and, generally, a place where a man could consume cheap alcohol and collapse in a state of near drunken paralysis at very little cost to the wallet. Those dances, where young teenagers were able to attend, had many protocols that had to be strictly adhered to. Men and young lads would be required to line up on one side of the dancehall at the commencement of the evening's entertainment provided by a local showband and eye up the females seated, or, standing at the other end of the dance floor. When sufficient courage was achieved, under the wary eyes of his colleagues a brave lad would make his way across the floor and politely request the pleasure of a dance with the chosen female.

"Do you want to dance?" would be the full extent of the breakthrough conversation from the nervous teenager.

"Naw, I'm waiting for someone else," she might respond if the targeted girl did not fancy him or just didn't like the cut of him when up close.

The return walk of shame and humiliation across the floor in front of the now giggling girls amidst the dancing couples was a slow and tortuous one especially, when all the other lads, who had crossed before, had successfully secured a dance with a girl. A rejection was hard to take, especially, if your acne was playing up and the blackheads were in abundance on the face. Novice young men soon had to learn the hard way if they wanted to attract a girl onto the dance floor with them. Confidence and a bit of cheek were the two key components for success. Walk brazenly across to the waiting femme fatales, stick out the left hand in the general direction of the intended partner and watch as she grabs the hand and you twirl her on to the floor like Fred Astaire on speed. Sadly, that was the theory but for me and most of my colleagues it seldom worked. On occasions a young lad might engage with a slightly older woman who would usually respond to such arrogance from an upstart with the words, "Sorry, I don't dance with a child." If brave enough, the response would be "Really sorry Miss, I didn't know you were pregnant," but you would need shedloads of courage and a swift body movement to avoid a hard slap on the face. Still the Foresters Hall on a Saturday evening was a lot of fun albeit with very little luck in obtaining that elusive snog.

Communities were divided along religious lines. Catholics would live in areas separate from their Protestant neighbours and more often than not in the low rental parts of the town. Very few Catholic families owned their properties and had to make do with whatever house or dwelling they could find within the meagre means. High levels of unemployment coupled with a burgeoning birth rate resulted in very few couples being able to purchase their own homes with the result that large families lived cheek by jowl in sub-standard accommodation. In our community, everyone knew each other including who was going out with whom so any success by a pubescent young man with a local girl was guaranteed to be headline news amongst the teenage population no later than the following morning. I knew her family since I was a toddler but when I turned 16, I fell in love with Eilish, one of a family of ten children who lived nearby. Sadly, the feeling was not reciprocated due to a number of factors. Although my pursuit of her was unrelenting she was not for turning or to use a local expression she was not on the pull. Eilish was 17, going on 18 and good looking. I had just turned 16 with a face covered in spots with the occasional blackhead to complement the acne. Spots on the forehead, spots on the nose and across the face and even spots on the arse not that she would ever see them. But I still fancied my chances.

Eilish was looking after her parents' shop one early mid-summer evening whilst the rest of the family were on their knees in the kitchen reciting the Rosary. This was an opportune time for me to woo her as the Rosary would usually take 20 minutes or so to complete and my chat-up lines were short. In fact, so short that they were just a couple of one-liners.

"How are things going, Eilish?" I said by way of a sexually charged opening line. My face starting to go ever so slightly rouge.

"Aye, not bad. What about you, Son?" She replied in hushed tones so as not to be heard over the mumbling in the kitchen. And she called me 'son', which was a bit of woeful start.

"Going really well, Eilish. You're looking good these days," as I continued to smooth talk her.

"Can I have a small bag of those gobstoppers please, Eilish?" as I continued to woo her and have her submit to my desires in the time it took her family to say the Rosary. She half-smiled. Sort of.

Eilish proceeded to fill the small bag with the multi-coloured gobstoppers using a little metal scoop.

"Is that sufficient for you?" showing me the half-filled bag.

"Aye, that's great, Eilish," as she twirled the top of the bag into a little half-knot.

"Ten pence," she replied as she held out her hand to take the money and this time there was a huge smile on her cute face. I could feel the passion rising within me.

"Thanks," I said, nonchalantly attempting to put the gobstoppers in my trouser pocket that by now had become surprisingly quite tight.

"Hmm, Eilish," I half mumbled.

"What is it? Do you want something else?" she replied in a husky voice. I leant forward and could smell the waft of her recently washed hair. I was in there.

"Don't suppose, you would like to go out with me sometime, maybe the pictures, one evening." I blathered on even though I did not have the money to entertain her to the front seats in the County Cinema never mind the extra legroom chairs at the rear.

"What age are you now, pray tell me, Son?" she replied without taking her eyes off the little blackhead that was quietly festering on the tip of my red nose which I could now feel starting to glow with embarrassment.

"I'm 16, sort of Eilish. But I am big for my age, honestly," half mumbling as my face seemed as if was about to combust it was so red and hot but I couldn't help myself. The palms of my hands felt as if little rivulets of sweat were dripping through my fingertips. She looked directly into my eyes and gently shook her head.

"Well, come back when you are 18 and if those spots have gone, you never know your luck, Son," she replied giggling. And then winked at me in a sultry sort of way. I winked in return, but both my eyes closed simultaneously resembling more like a blink rather than a wink.

I bid my adieu, turned on my heels and with spots glowing like a distress beacon I exited the shop. Heartbroken. With one last glance over my shoulder, I saw her standing there looking at me as I walked away and I could just see a broad smile that filled her lovely face. I still loved Eilish, even though she had refused the romantic advances of a prepubescent but dashing unwashed young Casanova. I had intended to return to my wooing of her when I turned 18, but it was not to be. Years later, I heard that after she qualified as a nurse in the local County Hospital, Eilish had met and married some nice local lad who was spot-free and they had lots of children together. It should have been me though. Shite!

A Close Encounter

There was one glorious occasion when I had an evening's encounter who had been a pupil at the local Loreto Convent. She had just passed her A levels and was on her way to study for a degree at the prestigious Queens University in Belfast. We met when I was sitting on a wall near her home on the Derry Road, a few hundred yards from our house. When I first said hello to her as she walked by, she smiled at me. A real gushing smile on her plump face. Lots of teeth. She seemed to hesitate, looked back in my general direction and then slowly returned to where I was sitting on the wall, which she suggestively leant against so that she was looking up at me. I could tell that we had a lot in common. She had seriously bad spots. Even worse spots than I had. But no blackheads though, which was a bonus. My learned friend, John, who would later become something important in the St John's Ambulance Brigade and would tend to the medical needs of people who collapsed at football matches or at various parades in the town, once told me that girls did not have blackheads as it was something to do with their DNA. He never told me what DNA was so I was none the wiser and just accepted his sage advice. Anyway, I never thought then that girls could get blackheads as my sister was clear skinned with only the occasional spot on her forehead and that it was only daft horny boys who were covered in them. One morning after 10 'clock Mass at the Sacred Heart when the neighbours convened for the daily gossip Mrs Fullerton, who had given birth to a large number of young ones and was well versed in all things medical except how to remove varicose veins, announced that spots emanated directly from eating too much chocolate. To my horror, Cassie Ann agreed with her and from that day onwards, I was banned from eating chocolate in the house. It wasn't even Lent for heaven's sake. The one consolation was that I could still eat chocolate outside the home and she would not have a clue. There was just one problem though. I never had that much money to buy any chocolate.

Anyway, this girl who was about to go to university and had lots of spots, was called Siobhan, as in 'shove on your knickers, your mammy is coming'. Of course, I did not actually say so such to Siobhan although I suspected that she knew what everyone said about a girl whose name is Siobhan. After some casual banter, Siobhan suggested that I take her to the cinema the following Saturday evening. Just like that. Completely out of the blue and I had not even made the first move. I had pulled. My very first ever real-life snogging partner-to-be. From now on I was to be known as the Don Juan of the Derry Road. Finally, I had physically got off with a girl, even if she had more spots on her face than I had. A real girl with lumpy bits under her jumper. I hurriedly accepted her suggestion of a date at the Pictures. Would have been madness not to say yes. In a casual sort of way and not seeming to be too eager. 'Oh Jesus, of course, I will. County Cinema it is then this Saturday evening', I responded. A little too much gushing possibly but I did not think I gave it away that I was really keen. Siobhan smiled just enough so that I could see her lovely off-white teeth glowing in the autumn sunshine.

Next Saturday it was to be, Siobhan. You lucky girl. Long walks, non-stop kissing and holding hands. God I was in Heaven. Love and lust were within my grasp with my first ever girlfriend-to-be the wonderful Siobhan. Later I simply floated home my feet not touching the ground.

We arranged to meet at the top of the hill on the Derry Road that Saturday evening. Although just far enough out of sight of our house in case Cassie Ann was on the lookout for loose girls chasing her favourite son. I had attempted to remove the few bits of bum hair from my chin with my father's razor and really scrubbed my face until some of the spots started to bleed. The Izal toilet paper was not a great absorbent especially for slithers of pus and blood so I had to borrow a handkerchief from my sister's room to stem the bleeding. My plan was to walk the half-mile or so to the local picture house together with my delightful girlfriend in the hope that some of my friends might be out and about and clock that I had pulled. There was a problem though. The perennial shortage of money, of course. When I approached my Da for the cost of admission, he offered me an amount that was just sufficient for only my ticket. I pleaded with him for some more. He asked why and when I hesitantly told him the full story about my forthcoming date the wonderful man promptly smiled, reached into his trouser pocket and gave me the full amount for two tickets to the cinema and enough for a large bag of chips from Jack Garrity's Chip Shop on the way home. My Da was the king that afternoon. Of course, it would have been pointless asking

Cassie Ann for money to take a girl out as she thought it was immoral and downright sinful for 'that sort of nonsense'.

We met up at the top of the hill as arranged and she looked just gorgeous in her high-neck jumper and a long skirt down to her ankles. As for me, I had my hair neatly brushed, face scrubbed, blackheads popped and had brushed my teeth for ages with the new Colgate toothpaste that my older sister used to hide from us at the back of the big knicker drawer in her bedroom. Siobhan and I strolled slowly into town enjoying the warmth of that balmy summer's evening. I was nervous and was constantly looking around to catch sight of any of my friends who would be so jealous. Typical. Just when you need your friends they are nowhere to be seen.

I paid for two tickets to the big double seats at the back of the cinema and settled down to watch the romantic thriller—that's what it was billed as on the poster outside the main entrance. The two words 'romantic and thriller' perfectly suited the occasion. The evening just could not be better for thus handsome young man and his first real conquest, the luscious Siobhan. For the next hour and 50 minutes I made several attempts to put my right arm around her shoulders, but she shrugged me off as she said that I was distracting her concentration of the film. I even attempted a handhold but was met with a brush off as well. When the tedious film finally ended with the death of the female co-star the credits began to roll followed by the usual mad dash for the exit just before the commencement of the obligatory playing of the National Anthem – the English one of course. At the time there was some obscure law or legal obligation that required cinemagoers to stand for the duration of the rendition of the 'Queen', as it was locally known, but nobody had any notion of standing apart from a few Protestants who thought it was their patriotic duty. The one benefit of the playing of the 'Queen' was to waken a few drunks who had been enjoying a nice kip for a few hours in the comfort of the cinema.

As we wandered past Jack's Chip Shop near the Sacred Heart Church, Siobhan suggested that we should buy some chips for the walk home. An extra-large bag was her request. When she said 'we', she meant me, of course. Problem was that I only had enough money for her extra-large bag of chips and not enough left over for my small bag of Jack's fabulous cut spuds that always tasted divine, especially with lots of vinegar and too much salt. Jack looked at me as he was taking the payment and for a split-second, I think he realised that I was not going to be a recipient of any of his fine chips even though the bag was crammed with them. Jack could see that my date for the night was a big girl and very probably had a healthy appetite especially for his finger-licking chips. He was seldom wrong.

Siobhan offered me a chip or two from her bag as we strolled home to her house in an estate several hundred yards past our house on the Derry Road. I declined her kind invitation for a couple of chips with the excuse that I wasn't hungry as I had a big dinner earlier. In actual fact I was absolutely starving but passed up the opportunity of grabbing a handful in case it made me look greedy.

She smiled and proceeded to devour the lot and threw the empty bag over her shoulder into some bushes that we passed on the way to her house. When we arrived at the corner of the street where she lived, we stood quietly under the shadow of the streetlight. I could feel the tension in the air and had great expectations. She glanced up at me with her beautiful bluish-grey eyes, her lips still sticky and salty from the greasy chips and burped. "Thanks for the lovely evening." She promptly turned on her heels and quickly disappeared into the darkness. I stayed there for a minute or two, scratching my nether regions and thinking to myself how cruel girls could be especially when it came to eating chips and not even as much as a quick snog. After a while, I slowly walked back up the hill and quietly let myself in with Daddy's key. Cassie Ann was in bed but Felix was sitting in the kitchen beside the range smoking a Players cigarette.

"Well, how did it go, Son?"

"Ach, not bad, Daddy," I replied not meeting his eyes.

"Did you get a wee kiss from whatever her name is?" He inquired as he leant forward towards me on the couch with his black mongrel dog busily licking its testicles beside him.

"I'm off to bed, Daddy. See you in the morning." My face felt like the colour of beetroot.

"Ah, well, don't you worry your head, Cub. There's plenty more of those fish in the sea and you won't be short of them, mark you my words, Son. Now, off to bed with you and don't forget to say your prayers. You have Mass in the morning so get a good night's sleep." I did not sleep very well, to be honest.

And that was my first real encounter with the opposite sex. Not even a kiss and me having scrubbed my teeth in the expectation of an evening of endless passion and snogging. I had even practised my snogging abilities in front of the bathroom mirror but all to no avail. Siobhan returned to Queens University in Belfast that Autumn and picked up a first-class Honours degree in Psychology which was not a surprise to me since she was a very bright individual especially as she obviously saw me coming a mile off that night at the County Cinema. Subsequently, I heard she was married with a houseful of young ones and living somewhere in England.

She still owes me for that extra-large bag of chips from Jack's Chippie on that fruitless, snog-free hot and very bothered balmy evening so many years ago.

Girls were really difficult to meet where we lived. Schools across the country were completely segregated along religious grounds and in the case of the Catholic grammar schools, they were single-sex only. The Catholic schools were all maintained meaning that the Church paid for the buildings and their upkeep and the cost of employing the lay teachers. The Protestant schools were state-run and well managed but were not answerable to any religious organisation, although, they did say their prayers. Rugby, cricket and hockey pitches were provided for those fortunate youngsters attending the latter whilst the Catholics had to make do with a couple of cow fields that were converted into playing surfaces for Gaelic football and hurling. This last-named sport is also known as a game for country cousins due to the level of aggression and violence demonstrated by the participants. Big strong country boys know how to wield a hurling stick on the playing fields much better than their town counterparts. And if a boy was proficient with a hurling stick or had shown prospects of being a half-decent Gaelic footballer, he was spared the usual daily thuggery from the Christian Brothers. Unfortunately, my abilities with a hurling stick were seldom witnessed on the pitch and consequently the relentless beatings from the thuggish clerics continued unabated.

To this day, most schools in the country are still segregated with children from both communities given little opportunity to mix either academically or socially. Thus, the division continues alongside the bigotry and hatred for each other's religious beliefs. But we are good Christians, nonetheless. Just not all the time.

The Arms

The Royal Arms was the entertainment centre of that small town at the weekends. The venue was owned by an enterprising man by the name of Dai Watterson who would arrange for huge stars to come from England and perform in his provincial dancehall. The likes of Tom Jones and Engelbert Humperdinck graced the stage singing to adoring young audiences who were crammed tight into the hall from door to stage with little or no room for dancing. To see such stars up close in our little town was a dream come true.

The Arms was also the dancehall in which to be seen on a Saturday night. That is providing you had the money to afford the entrance fee and the price of a few drinks. Sadly, as 17 and 18-year-olds, money was tight or non-existent; therefore, admission to the dances was a rarity. My summer job in the local co-op only paid a few pounds which was paltry especially after having to share half with Cassie Ann.

"There's nothing for nothing in this world, cub," she would say as I would hand over the money every Saturday evening after work.

We would meet in a friend's house late Saturday evening or sit five-handed around a plate of chips in the Golden Griddle and discuss our plan of attack to gain entry to the Arms ballroom and access to all those good-looking girls who would be desperate for such good-looking boys. Our weekly strategy was always a variation of the same tactics. Late into the evening we would loiter just outside the entrance to the hall, usually sitting on a couple of the nearby windowsills whilst keeping watch on the two bouncers in the hope of a fight breaking out. Fights were a regular occurrence, especially when big strong country lads consumed enough alcohol and subsequently engaged with the local townies with whom there was very little love lost.

When the inevitable row broke out in the ballroom, the bouncers would quickly move in to identify the culprits and escort them to the exit by hurling them down the steep flight of stairs and eject them on to the street where the willing doormen would ensure that the troublemakers would be reluctant to return. Whilst the doormen were engaged in fisticuffs with the various protagonists, we would quietly make our way past the melee, rush up the stairs two at a time and merge into the crowd of dancers. For all intents and purposes, we would simply appear to be onlookers and drinkers who were part of the ensemble from the beginning. The next stage of the plan was to obtain alcohol. As we were potless, the only option left open to us was to watch for those groups of lotharios heading in the direction of the women gathered at the far side of the hall in the hope of being asked for a dance thereby leaving their drinks unattended. This would provide us with the opportunity to casually wander past the temporarily vacated table that was stacked high with drink and help ourselves to a few half-finished glasses of anything remotely drinkable and, if lucky, a neat whiskey or a vodka. Drink in hands, we would then move further up the hall trying to look innocent whilst gulping down the alcohol.

It was a great plan and one that we always enjoyed. Stealing someone's drinks was a dangerous occupation however but when successful our spirits, with as many as possible inside our guts, were well and truly lifted. But the thieving of drinks was not without its risk. On one occasion, a member of our gang of alcohol thieves, Jim, who was a few years older than the rest of us and in his first year at the Catholic teachers' training college in Belfast, was too brave in his quest for half-finished drinks. With great aplomb or foolhardiness, he would saunter up to a table occupied by a couple enjoying a drunken embrace and relieve them of their glasses and wander off into the crowd. Unfortunately, there were times when he was caught in the act of lifting a glass from a table by the owner and would promptly receive a swift smack in the face resulting in a bloody nose. Such ignominy never deterred the man though.

"Just one of the hazards of my profession," was always Jim's response, when we eventually picked him up from the floor and helped him on to a seat.

Those Saturday nights, when we were unable to breach the bouncer's lines, we would sit on the windowsills near the entrance of that Ballroom of Romance and ogle at the couples exiting the hall, with their arms wrapped around their girlfriends for the night. Invariably, they would look upon us with a degree of pity and throw us a wink as they nonchalantly walked past. Girls, who should have been on our arms were now with lads of our own age and we just sat and watched and mumbled obscenities. After the last of the revellers had departed and the bouncers had closed the large double doors, we would wander off to Jim's house where we would drink weak tea and discuss at great length how life had been so cruel to us. At 5 am as the sun was rising our romantic futures did indeed look bleak. But, at least, we had Mass the following morning to look forward to. In just a few short few hours we would be at prayer in the Sacred Heart. No matter what our behaviour, girls or no girls, attendance at weekly Mass was not to be missed in our household. There were times when I wished I could just lie in bed on a Sunday morning and think of girls instead of having to traipse up the hill to pray for the forgiveness of so many sins that I would have just loved to have committed but never had an opportunity to enjoy.

She was a deeply religious woman. Cassie Ann loved being a Catholic and attended 10 0'Clock Mass most mornings with Rosary Beads intertwined through her calloused hands. During the Holy Months of May and October, when the Blessed Virgin, the Mother of Christ was honoured, she was in her usual pew for every daily 10 O'clock Mass. Cassie Ann could always be found seated at the back of the Sacred Heart Church with her constant companion, the black mongrel dog called Bonny with a white blaze on its forehead, lying at her feet and constantly fiddling with its nether regions and farting profusely. Not for her the daily ritual of parading up to the front of the sacred altar in her finest as was the wont of some of the local dignitaries' wives. Indeed not. Cassie Ann knew her station in that holy place of worship. Mind you she possessed very little of what could be described as *'finery'* with which to strut and show off at Mass. Same coat and same hat for every Mass was her attire. Any money that came her way was spent on her children and never on her. Vanity was not a sin that she could ever be accused of. And her seat was at the back of the church where she felt most comfortable and the least exposed.

Unless it was a matter of life and death, to miss Sunday Mass was to commit a mortal sin. Her soul would burn in the raging fires of Hell for evermore if she was unable to attend the weekly ritual. The priests knew who came to each of the four Sunday morning Masses and would notice if a regular was missing.

Teenagers would be quizzed by their parents after Mass, as to the identity of the Priest celebrating the ceremony that they were supposed to have attended just in case they had tried to skip it and disappear with their friends for the morning. And woe betide him or her if their lies were ever found out. Skipping Mass and then lying about it was a punishable offence.

Mass was always celebrated by the Priest in Latin, also known as the Tridentine Mass. It was not until 1970 that an enlightened Pope Paul VI decided that Latin was not the first language of most of the world's Catholics and declared that it should be celebrated in the local language of each country. In the Sacred Heart Church, very few members of the congregation had ever been taught Latin at school but they all knew the words of the Mass nonetheless and, parrot fashion, they would say whatever was required during the service. The Priest, in his resplendent vestments, that were usually violet in colour or occasionally cream and lavishly decorated with ornate designs depending upon the Feast Day, would stand facing the altar with his back to the crowd of worshippers. The Missal or prayer book contained all the Latin text that the congregation were required to follow assiduously. There were also many worshippers who had memorised the words, including Cassie Ann, who could recite the entire Mass in Latin including those parts reserved for the Priest without ever referring to the Missal.

When it came to that part of the Mass when the Priest was required to preach to the audience about their wickedness and sinful ways, he would walk the short distance to the highly decorated Pulpit close to the nave and would slowly climb the stairs as if it was a state occasion and then face his eagerly awaiting congregation. By tradition, the Pulpit from the Latin Pulpitum meaning platform or staging, was raised well above the floor so that the speaker could be seen and most definitely could be heard, with or without a microphone. The Priest with his well-manicured nails on nicotine-stained fingers that were just visible as they dangled from the white surplice of his sleeves, would glare at the congregation as he prepared to speak. It was as if the entire audience had spent the previous week committing unspeakable sins and it was now his duty to remind them of their wickedness. He would grip the red velvet covering the upper surround of the Pulpit and would lean forward menacingly as he commenced his sermon to the expectant flock of sinners gazing up at him from their packed pews. Sometimes, reading from notes, he would quote passages from the various Acts of the Apostles. In the case of those under 25 years of age in the audience these lectures were about as relevant as a fart in Neil Armstrong' spacesuit. None of us knew or cared where Damascus was and frankly, we were not that bothered either if a young Jewish lad, with the unlikely Yiddish name of Paul, suddenly had a Damascene insight into something worthwhile whilst meandering down a dusty road in the Middle East. For most of the time, we would sit there trying not to look bored and being more concerned about how long we had to sit listening to endless parables and trying desperately hard not to fall asleep. Or indeed trying to avoid having bad thoughts about those good-looking girls who would be sitting on the long bench in front of the council estate on the Derry Road later that afternoon. And the remote possibility, however unlikely, of having a snog with the lovely Susie, she of the amazing frontal bits.

The church would be packed to overflowing at each of the four Sunday Masses. Some of the male congregation, however, would stand in the vestibule at the back of the church so that they could make a quick exit as soon as Communion was half-way over and before the Priest commenced saying the final prayers. Communion would take ages as most of the congregation would line up to take the blessed host from the Priest, who would be attended by his altar boys in their white vestments over red tunics, holding a silver salver under the chin of each recipient in case the host dropped from the mouth. An early escape was not always possible. A few of the more devout priests had become disgruntled at the hurried exit from Mass especially, if they had not even started the final prayers. To curtail or prevent such disrespectful behaviour a curate would patrol the entrance to the Church to ensure that all attendees would stay put to the bitter end especially those who were desperate for a few puffs on a Woodbine or Players cigarette. Invariably it was Father Gestapo himself, the Brylcreem-gelled Father Clerkin who would creep around the permitter of the front doors of the Church and forcibly usher those lingering at the entrance into any available pew nearby. If it meant walking these reluctant Catholics halfway up the centre aisle for every good parishioner to gaze upon them with contempt or possibly manhandle them into the rear of the church, the enthusiasm of Clerkin was unrelenting. On other occasions latecomers would simply be blocked from entry by the self-appointed bouncer and forcibly reminded to return well before the commencement of the following Mass. There was always the exception. Some of the more respected and well-off members of the flock who would make it a habit of being a few minutes late for each 10 am Mass irrespective of whether it was the Parish Priest or a lowly curate who was the celebrant. One such individual was a very portly local solicitor, who was a significant benefactor to the Church as well as being the legal adviser to the clergy, would arrive at the front door of the church in the latest model of whatever car he was driving and together with his wife would stroll into Mass even when it was well under way. Like a modern-day Uriah Heap, Father Clerkin would stand to attention whilst opening the car doors for the dignitary and his well-fed wife and greet them with much bowing and scraping. Mr Portly Solicitor, wearing his best Sunday suit and desperately trying to cover his relentlessly expanding waistline, would accompany his well-dressed wife wearing an expensive fur overcoat and thick stockings that could not disguise the numerous varicose veins on the back of her legs, up the centre aisle where they would take their reserved seats in the front pew. A quick nod to the Priest from Mr Portly by way of an apology for any inconvenience and for the priest to continue celebrating Mass. The Catholic Church was a broad church and welcomed all comers but most especially those who had money. And if a man had money and was a Catholic, Sunday Mass was the perfect place to demonstrate your Christianity, your love of your fellow practitioners and your wealth.

"Would you look at the pair son. Stuck up heathens the pair of them." was always Cassie Ann's comment upon seeing the two of them as the paraded their wealth to a packed church of impoverished, hungry commoners.

On a rare occasion, the Priest might say something that would catch our attention. The Civil Rights movement was beginning to attract lots of attention from local and international media and our tiny country was now gradually moving in a direction that might just mean that there would be equality of sorts for all its people and not just one section of the community. Preaching politics from the Pulpit was usually frowned by the hierarchy of the Catholic Church but, on occasions, a young Priest with a social conscience, would make references to the violence that would eventually engulf so many towns and villages and destroy so many lives, innocent or otherwise. Father McCloskey was such a man. He was diplomatic with how he would phrase his criticism of the government that ruled the country and would never flinch from denouncing any violent acts against innocent people whether they were Protestant or Catholic. Father McCloskey had gained the respect and admiration of the young men and women in the congregation and when he would first appear on the altar to say Mass, the faces of the young ones would light up with anticipation about what he was about to preach from the Pulpit. He did not last long in the Parish. After an unusually short few years as a curate, an honourable and thoughtful individual who was popular with his flock and tended to our spiritual needs, and even made us laugh, was off without so much as a farewell sermon and an opportunity to say goodbye. The Catholic Church was not a great supporter of revolutionary clerics in their midst although the Spanish Civil War did attract many young men wearing clerical collars to fight for the cause of the Republic. Father McCluskey might have been one of those priests at such a time but he was not permitted to linger in our small town long enough for us young ones to find out.

When I was aged six, Cassie Ann began to educate me on how I should prepare for my Holy Communion. This is a rite of passage for all young Catholics and entails confessing your sins to the Priest and seeking absolution. From an early age youngsters are required to enter a tall box in the church which has a red-velvet covered narrow entrance on each side. This is known as the Confessional Box where the youngster is required to kneel on a padded cushion to await the opening of a hatch through which the priest would bark out his demands. The expectation was that the child would tell his confessor all about the multitude of venial and mortal sins he or she had committed during the previous week. Six-year-old boys have a very loose grasp of right and wrong at such a young age but Cassie Ann knew how to satisfy the sin-hungry, hungover clergyman and what he wanted to hear. After all we are sinners and the priest was appointed by God to hear and forgive our wicked ways.

"Tell him, you stole some money from my purse," she said. "You will only get three Hail Marys and a Glory Be to the Father for that. Then say an Act of Contrition, bless yourself and you are forgiven."

"I never stole money from your purse Mammy." I replied, my eyes filling with tears.

"Never mind about that son. I know you didn't steal any money but the priest needs to hear you confess to a sin before he can forgive you. Do you not understand that, for heaven's sake? Pretend you have sinned and he will forgive you."

"Alright, Mammy. I will tell him I took money from your purse that you hide behind that wee statue of a white dog on the mantelpiece."

"That's a good boy,'" as she gently patted my head.

"How much will I tell him I stole from your purse, Mammy?"

"Get in there you wee shite and be quick about it. I have my shopping to do in the co-op," she replied as she rubbed the back of her left leg, the one with the worst of the varicose veins.

She was right, of course. When I told the priest about my wickedness, he nodded in such a way as if he had heard the same sin a thousand times from so many children and with that, he gave me absolution with a slight flicker of impatience and a whiff of stale alcohol.

"Three Hail Marys, now go and sin no more, my child. And say an Act of Contrition." he whispered but just loud enough for the old biddies waiting outside in the pews for their turn to tell all to the priest about their wickedness, whether actual or imagined. "O my God, I am heartily sorry for having offended thee and I detest my sins above every other evil." I finished my Contrition even though I hardly understood a word of it, made the Sign of the Cross and hurried out of the scary confessional box. I knelt beside my mother who was in the pew directly opposite the Confessional to say my Hail Marys and felt her arm gently rubbing my back. That was my first confession. And my first public admission of a crime of which I was innocent. Many more private sins, more mortal than venial, were to follow during the years ahead.

Making one's Confession was a weekly requirement for the young and the old in the Parish. Friday evenings were a favourite time to attend as there were many priests eagerly waiting to hear the multiple sins of the local people and to bestow forgiveness upon those errant and wicked creatures. Parishioners who wished to make their confession would take their place in a pew and form an orderly queue to enter the dark and foreboding Confessional Box. The Priest, if he was not in the best of form, or desperate for a large whisky or two, would impatiently listen to the sins of the faithful followed by their rendition of the Act of Contrition and then dish out a harsh penance if he thought their sins were really bad. The hatch between the confessor and the confessed would be quickly shut and finally on to the next sinner. The Penitent or absolved sinner, now free from his or her sins, would exit the box with head down whilst desperately trying to avoid the ever-watchful eyes of those awaiting to take their turn behind the heavy dark purple velvet curtains. All was now forgiven until the next visit to the Confessional Box, the following week.

On rare occasions, one of the local curates would visit our house in Brook Street to pray with, and for, Cassie Ann. We were poor and not deserving of such visits but our GP, Doctor Bill McMullan, who cared for my mother, had suggested that it would be an act of kindness for a priest to pay a visit to one of their flock from time to time. Father Devine was an aged priest and one who had enjoyed the many comforts of his calling. From the breadth of his girth and the reddening of his nose, he was a man that demonstrably knew how to enjoy the life of a well-heeled cleric. The poor were an unnecessary burden in his parish but as God's chosen one on this blessed earth, he felt obliged, occasionally, to visit the sick and dying and offer a few hurried words of comfort. And then on to the golf club for his next tee time.

"Your mother is not well, but with God's help she will recover," he would tell us frightened children huddled together around the open fire in the front room after his brief visit with her in the bedroom.

"I have heard her confession just now and we prayed together for her forgiveness from the good Lord above," he pronounced with great pomposity whilst still wearing his purple stole.

"Life can be cruel," he continued, "But if we pray every morning and every evening your mummy will recover. Mark you my words."

Father Devine didn't look as if life had been too cruel to him over the years. Especially, with his bulbous red nose, rotund belly and the new car gleaming in the early evening sun outside our front door, the only vehicle in the street. It would take many years before Cassie Ann would fully recover from the trauma that robbed us of her for so long. And no thanks to the local clergy and their prayers.

The Catholic Church luxuriates in rituals. Lots of them. One 'not to be missed' ritual for all young boys and girls as they approach their teenage years is the requirement to undertake the Confirmation ceremony. This is compulsory as failing to do means that one cannot be considered a fully-fledged functioning Catholic. This archaic rite of passage is not dissimilar to the Jewish Bar Mitzva ceremony where the young man enters Jewish adulthood thereby becoming a full member of the adult congregation. Except that girls are not allowed.

Receiving Confirmation entails the conferring of an additional Christian name by the Bishop of the Diocese, a name that your Mummy would choose without any discussion or argument. There was no messing with the chosen name. It had to be a Christian one and preferably one associated with a canonized saint or some hero from the New Testament although Samson and Delilah were a definite no. And most certainly there was to be no Eliza or Robbie or other such fashionable forenames. And definitely none of those awful Protestant names such as Henry, William, or Elizabeth.

The ceremony consisted of standing or kneeling in front of some overfed and over-the-top dressed pompous bishop wearing a Mitre on his balding head and red vestments draped around his torso so as to symbolise the red tongues of fire as seen hovering over the heads of the apostles at Pentecost. Pure theatre in a church setting. This was my first real introduction to showbusiness in the Catholic Church. The bishop would anoint the chosen victim using a dab of Chrism, a consecrated oil, to make the Sign of the Cross on the recipient's forehead whilst saying your Confirmation name and "Be sealed with the gift of the Holy Spirit." And to really rub it in, the unfortunate individual would then be required to kiss the bishop's outsize ring, the ultimate humiliation. It was more like a scene from a drag show rather than the bestowal of the Sacrament of Confirmation on some reluctant teenager.

We were told, or constantly reminded, that the recipients of Confirmation received a special grace by which our faith was deepened and strengthened and that as good Christians, we would begin to see more clearly our responsibilities in life. They never mentioned that this responsibility meant we could now throw stones and bricks at the soldiers and the Royal Ulster Constabulary whenever an opportunity arose. Or indeed how to get off with the lovely Susie from Gallows Hill.

A little-known ceremony that was also practised by the Catholic Church as recently as the late 1950s was the cleansing and forgiveness of the souls of those women parishioners who had recently given birth. The Church had always insisted that sex, a word never to be heard emanating from the mouth of a priest, was the essential element of the marital act which is intrinsically connected with procreation. In layman's words it simply means that couples should indulge in sexual activities only if they wish to have babies. Enjoyment of that union was forbidden. Indeed, sexual shenanigans were deeply frowned upon by the Catholic clergy. As for contraception that was banned with absolutely no exceptions, even if the unfortunate mother already had given birth to multiple children with little or no means to feed them. After 10 or 11 children, the joy of sex must have waned for most poor Catholic mothers.

The ceremony to cleanse the mother, after the birth of her latest child, entailed attending a special blessing in the church where only women would be present. The Priest would beckon the new mother to the altar and there he would forgive her for any enjoyment that she may have experienced with her husband during the creation of the infant. It was an unwritten rule that Catholic women should just lie back and think of Rome whilst their husbands enjoyed themselves on top or behind the unfortunate wife. The practice of cleansing ceased many years ago, but Cassie Ann had been a frequent visitor to the Sacred Heart after so many of her births, both for those who lived and for those less fortunate ones who did not survive.

Catholicism had the Nationalist population of Ireland in its ever-tightening grip for many centuries. Sex was solely for procreation and never ever for enjoyment between a married man and his wife. A quick drunken poke of the unwilling wife and another unwelcome mouth to feed arrives nine months later would suffice. Some of the local women would have up to 10 or 12 children whilst living in a two-bedroom little house with an outdoor toilet and only a concrete job box to wash the weans and the clothes. Asking a priest for advice on contraception was never a good idea. 'It's in God's Hands' was the usual reply. It certainly was not in the hands of the women of Ireland.

Pat O'Neill was a few older than us and was a man whom we looked up to in many ways. He was wise like his father, who was active in local politics, and attracted lots of girls, unlike the rest of us. He was someone whom we could trust implicitly. One evening we all met for a chat as he was seeking our collective support ahead of a visit to the confessional box the following Saturday morning, the day when the older members of the parish confessed their sins. Pat informed us that he sinned 'big time' and needed to confess to a priest and to seek his forgiveness. However, he wanted to make sure that he would not be interrogated too much by one of the younger priests so a plan was formed whereby he would seek to join the queue for the aged and very deaf priest who would fall asleep on occasions. To him he would quietly admit his crime of passion and seek forgiveness. For this Pat required our moral support because what he was about to confess was 'monumental'. We just could not wait for Saturday morning and his confession of wickedness whatever it was.

As previously agreed, we met outside the Sacred Heart Church with a worried looking Pat on that fateful Saturday morning. He looked nervous and was really anxious about what was to befall him in the minutes ahead. We were not aware of the sin he was about to confess, but it was obviously of such magnitude that there would be grave consequences for this unfortunate sinner. We walked into the Church from the Castle Street entrance and deposited ourselves, all six of us, on the pew nearest the Confessional Box where the old deaf priest was usually located. Several old cronies were sitting nearby, Rosary Beads twirling in their hands, and occasionally glancing in our general direction eyeing us up as if we were up to no good. They knew that we should have confessed our sins the previous evening as all decent young men and women of the town did so they were wary of us. We avoided any eye contact. When it was Pat's turn to enter that cabinet of sinfulness, he looked towards us for the spiritual support we had promised. We winked and nodded our approval as he pulled back the heavy velvet curtain and disappeared out of sight.

As one, we lent in the direction of the confessional box and desperately tried to hear the details of his admission of whatever the dreadful sin of which he was guilty. It was very quiet, at first and we could barely hear a word. Then we recognised the priest's voice. Shite. It was not the doddery old deaf one but that curate from Hell, Father Longnose Clerkin.

"You touched her where?" We could clearly hear the anger in his voice. We could not hear Pat's response.

"She is from where?" This time even louder from the priest. Again, near silence from Pat.

"A Protestant. You mean to tell me you were out with a Protestant and you touched her private bits?" he shouted.

Hearing these words, the old ladies looked at each other and began making repeated Signs of the Cross. We glanced at each other and then started to giggle. Who was this Protestant hussy? And where indeed did she live? And has she any friends with whom might become attached? Sitting there in the Catholic Church, that Holy place, our thoughts just ran wild in anticipation of meeting some of this girl's Protestant friends.

Pat finally exited the Confessional Box. He looked pale and frightened. We watched him as he walked towards the altar and knelt before it and commenced praying. He had just been awarded one of the highest penalties that a Confessor could hand down. A full Rosary consisting of fifty Hail Marys, ten Our Fathers and all the other bits in between. We passed up our turn to enter the Confessional Box and quickly exited the Church before the outraged priest appeared looking for yet more miscreants who enjoyed the company of teenage Protestant girls. Twenty minutes later Pat. He refused to elaborate on the identity of his erstwhile girlfriend, the one who had seduced him into doing dreadful things. We begged him but he would not budge. That secret would remain between him and the man in the Confessional Box. It was to be Pat's last ever confession.

Preacher Man

Every Saturday evening, a giant of a man in a gleaming white clerical collar would stand in the centre of the town surrounded by handful of Union Jack flag waving followers. For what seemed like ages he would screech through a loudhailer his hatred for all things Roman Catholic and especially that devil-worshipping Pope in Rome whom he referred to as the Antichrist. Eyes bulging with rivulets of spittle flying from the corners of his large mouth, indiscriminately spraying those standing nearby, he would rant and rage against all things Catholic, Rome, the evils of alcohol and homosexuals. As dusk set in his large protruding teeth would appear to glisten. The homosexual aspect of his ranting was a bit of a revelation to us teenagers. Those Saturday evenings we would cluster together to listen and shout abuse at this strange beast of a man and wonder why he such a hatred of so many things especially homosexuals. We checked with each other if anyone knew a homosexual but no names were forthcoming. We even checked a dictionary to make absolutely sure what was meant as 'homosexual' and thought little of it. But the mad preacher had obviously encountered homosexuals on his travels and he was not a big fan. Whatever their sexual predilections they were must have been as wicked as us Catholics.

With his Brylcreem-coated hair without any shadow of doubt this was a Bible-thumping preacher of the very old school. Over the years he had taken to the streets of the local towns and villages with a mission to warn his people, and anyone else who had the misfortune to be passing by, as to the evils of that man in the Vatican and his cohorts who he thought were all homosexuals. Catholicism was everywhere and it was contagious.

His followers would hand out copies of their weekly newspaper entitled 'The Protestant Telegraph', in which there were numerous articles about the wickedness of the Pope and his many children and of course, the evils of the Roman Catholic Church. The Preacher Man was ahead of his time in distributing free newspapers albeit, there were no advertisements other than requests for donations to his burgeoning church business and, of course, multiple quotes from the Bible.

The name of this Preacher Man was Doctor Ian Richard Kyle Paisley, aka Baron Bannside, Privy Councillor, to give him his full title. His doctorate was provided by a Bible college in the American south and did not rank with one granted by Harvard or even with a mail-order diploma. But still, he always referred to himself as 'Doctor'. He co-founded the fundamentalist Free Presbyterian Church of Ulster in 1951 and, subsequently, was its leader until 2008. Paisley became widely known for his hell and damnation sermons and regularly preached about and vehemently denounced Roman Catholicism, the Pope, ecumenism, homosexuality and anything or anyone who did not meet his high moral and religious Free Presbyterian standards. Whiskey was the Devil's brew and Satan's buttermilk and woe betide any of his followers who were not teetotal. His fiery brand of puritanism went down well with his devotees especially those living in rural communities who viewed him as something close to a Messiah. These supporters were known as Paisleyites, after the Big Man himself, although it was believed that the residents of Paisley in Scotland frowned upon their town being used to describe such extremist views.

He was a great rabble-rouser with many outlandish quotes attributed to him including the infamous one in 1969 when he said of Catholics: "They breed like rabbits and multiply like vermin." When Princess Margaret and the Queen Mother met Pope John XXIII in 1958, Paisley condemned them for 'committing spiritual fornication and adultery with the Antichrist'. He enjoyed poking fun at the Pope and when His Holiness Pope John died in June 1963, Paisley announced to a crowd of followers that, "This Romish man of sin is now in Hell." True to form Big Ian, as he was known to his beloved disciples, organised protests and the lowering of flags on public buildings to mark the Pope's death.

Paisley who was a relative nonentity since the mid-1960s, even before the return of the Troubles in 1968, eventually moved on from being a bit of an entertaining distraction, a clerical clown of sorts, to become a major divisive figure in the bitter and divided world of politics in Northern Ireland. His brand of violent political actions and hatred would dominate the country for many years. His Free Presbyterianism, he had his very own church, attracted many discontented Protestants who saw Big Ian as their salvation from all wickedness.

Paisley rapidly progressed up the toxic political landscape to become the First Minister of Northern Ireland. He also occupied a seat in the European Union, where he once interrupted the opening proceedings of the Parliament, to protest that the Union Jack flag outside the building was flying upside down. The female President at the time reminded the assembled MEPs that, as a mother of teenagers, she was well-used to coping with recalcitrant children. The other MEPs cheered wildly. Paisley went quiet for a short while. But not for long.

And this was the man who stood in the centre of our small town every Saturday evening, spewing out his bigotry and hatred to an amused audience of followers and sceptics alike. We enjoyed his mad ranting and we would simply laugh and walk off into the night. The Saturday evening drunks, staggering home from a day's drinking in the local pubs and gambling on the horses in the bookies, would gaze at Ian and his gang in wonderment and occasionally join in the singing much to the annoyance of the Big Man.

In the end, all that Paisley really wanted was recognition. From originally being viewed as a demented demagogue, he eventually became the man who ran Northern Ireland and a Lord of the Realm with a seat in the House of Lords. His venomous attacks on anyone opposing his politics eventually subsided and there are pictures of him laughing with the former IRA chief Martin McGuinness that earned them the nickname of the Chuckle Brothers. But for a very long time Paisley was no laughing matter.

I once told Cassie Ann about listening to this cartoon-like preacher and her response was, "Don't be talking to me about that creature. He's nothing but an Antichrist." From her response, I detected that there must have been an awful lot of Antichrists in Ireland at the time. I asked her about the ecumenism thing, but she said that she did not have the time to tell me as she had to go to Bingo in the Foresters Hall with Sadie from number 19 down the road.

Sadie was my mother's only Protestant friend in the neighbourhood although Sadie didn't practice any religion. They met through Bingo and became lifelong friends. Except on the 12th of July, each year when Protestant Orangemen would take to the streets across the Six Counties to commemorate the defeat of King James of Scotland by King William of Orange from Holland in a field beside the Boyne River in the Irish Republic in 1690. The Orange Order is exclusively Protestant and their members wear sashes and bowler hates when they march behind bands, pumping out loud music to annoy the Catholics. For their part, the Catholics disappear to Donegal for the day to avoid any confrontation until the parades finish and alcohol has taken its toll on the exhausted marchers. Sadie never marched behind any bands but would occasionally hang out a very small Union Jack from her top window. Sadie was just a proud Loyalist.

The Troubles

Cassie Ann was born close to the border in County Donegal, one of the twenty-six counties of the Irish Republic that had been finally liberated from the British in 1922. Politics did not exist for her rather it was a case of simply existing. On regular occasions, Cassie Ann and her mother would walk to Pettigo, the nearest village to the farm, where they would catch the steam train to Bundoran, some 30 miles down the coast in West Donegal. The reason for these journeys was not just to look at the Atlantic Ocean or to take a stroll around the gift shops that sold holy artefacts and cheap sweets but to purchase sugar, cigarettes and butter that they would secrete in their clothing and smuggle on the train back into the Northern side of the border and there sell their goods for a small profit.

The Customs Officers from the North would search all the men on board the trains when it was required to halt just inside the Northern Ireland border and would confiscate cigarettes or other illicit goods that were purchased in the Republic. But women were exempt as it was not considered appropriate to rifle through a woman's belongings for fear of causing offence. Cassie Ann and her mother always wore extra-large knickers and outsize bras for the illicit shopping expeditions to Donegal.

In the late 1960s, Catholics living in Northern Ireland were beginning to challenge the Protestant-run Government who controlled every aspect of life in the small Province. The responsibility for allocating social housing fell to local councillors who had been elected by house-owners in their constituency. Problem was that, very few Catholics owned their properties, thereby not having a vote and hence the Council was totally lopsided in favour of the Protestant population. By late 1968, several confrontations between students from Queens University in Belfast and the Royal Ulster Constabulary, the local police force that was drawn exclusively from the Protestant community, resulted in many arrests, internment without trial and eventually, the downward spiral into extreme violence that would continue for many years thereafter. Our town was no exception in that Nationalists were excluded from jobs, council houses and the right to vote in local elections, if they were not house owners. Lack of jobs meant that very few Catholics could afford their own property. The result was that most Nationalist families lived in inferior quality, over-crowded rented accommodation and until my father's redundancy, home for our family was a squalid, condemned by the council hovel located at the far end of Brook Street. We were the lucky ones; many were less fortunate.

Our house on the Derry Road was located directly opposite the living quarters for the families of the British soldiers who were stationed in the town. In the years that followed the ever-gregarious Cassie Ann developed a strong bond with many of the English wives for whom she felt some sympathy as they were living in a different country amongst people who resented their very presence. And whose accents they could barely understand and vice versa. She would invite them into our house for a cup of tea and a chat and even took them to Friday night bingo in the Foresters Hall, a Catholic community centre run by a society calling itself the Order of Irish National Foresters. I never did find out if any of the members of that august organisation ever worked in the local forests in the same way that Freemasons seldom laid bricks but it was a secret that they couldn't divulge to us mortals. In return for her hospitality, the wives would bring food rations from the barracks for Cassie Ann and they would spend evenings telling her about the towns and cities where they came from and what it was like to be a soldier's wife in a strange, foreboding land. Some of our neighbours frowned upon Cassie Ann's familiarity with the army wives, but none had the temerity to tell her to her face. One kind English army wife with a huge smile and a generous laugh had an accent that I eventually discovered originated in Lancashire. I would chat to her endlessly and ask her numerous questions about where she came from, the various football teams that played there and what it was like to live in her part of England and did they have the same problems of Catholics and Protestants hating each other as we did? Her name was Avril but Cassie Ann always referred to her as April, possibly because she had never met or heard of an Avril before. April, or Avril, depending on who was in the kitchen at the time, would bring little luxuries from the Army Naafi that we had never seen in the town. These would consist of gifts such as sweet-smelling soaps and bath fragrances which Cassie Ann lavished upon herself and the sister. It was very different from the carbolic soap that she would use to wash herself and her family when we lived in Brook Street.

The Civil Rights Movement took its lead from Martin Luther King in the United States and very soon Catholics were marching through towns and villages demanding parity with their Protestant neighbours and one man one vote. Sadly, violence ensued when the RUC decided that the marchers were no longer permitted to demonstrate and resorted to using batons and tear gas to ensure that the streets were kept clear of any disturbances. Tensions were raised as the Unionist politicians in Stormont reiterated their support for the Protestant RUC in quelling any unrest in the Nationalist community.

As the trouble spread throughout the North of Ireland across the road from our house the low walls surrounding the army barracks and the living quarters for the families were rapidly reinforced with high metal fences topped with barbed wire to protect the inhabitants from stone-throwing and petrol bomb attacks. Soldiers with camouflaged faces carrying assault rifles, started patrolling the town at all hours, stopping locals and demanding to know where they were going, their names and addresses and acting aggressively and keen for reactions. Young men and boys were subjected to full body searches and the occasional kicking or a thump from the butt of the rifle if they were belligerent or just plain unhelpful. Harmony with the resident battalion quickly dissipated. The soldier's wives stopped visiting and their Friday night bingo sessions ceased. Cassie Ann abhorred violence and knelt beside her bed each night to recite the Rosary in the hope that her young ones would not be dragged into the spreading turmoil. Her prayers were not to be answered.

One warm July afternoon after school had finished for the day, Cassie Ann sent me to the co-op shop near the centre of the town to purchase some butter. She had used the last of her supply earlier in the day, and a new batch was now needed to accompany the spuds that my father had with his dinner each and every evening. My Daddy loved butter with his spuds. However, a Civil Rights demonstration was in full flow and I and my packet of extra-large butter promptly joined my friends and fellow rebels in the front of the courthouse. Most of the demonstrators were young men and older boys, and it was decided by one of the ringleaders that the most appropriate method of annoying the police was for us all to sit in the middle of the road in the high street, the main thoroughfare, thereby blocking the traffic. Such action seemed sensible and quite exciting at the time, and without any hesitation, I joined my comrades in plonking my backside on the warm tarmac in the middle of the road.

There was great camaraderie with lots of singing of protest songs, the words of most I barely knew, but I mouthed along with everyone and thoroughly enjoyed the sense of rebellion. Meanwhile, the much-needed butter was not doing very well in the warm sunshine, and a plan was formed in my mind that I would make my excuses to the assembled crowd of protesters and hurry home in time for my father to lather his spuds with the rapidly melting yellow pulp. However, the plan did not work out as anticipated.

From the bottom of the High Street could be seen several RUC Land Rovers, weaving their way through the standing crowds and heading in the general direction of the seated protesters. The leader of our mini rebellion instructed us to remain seated on the ground which we did, reluctantly. Within a few minutes, we were unceremoniously picked up by less-than-friendly armed police officers and thrown on top of each other into the back of a Land Rover and driven at speed to the RUC barracks and there herded into cells. Sadly, I was not permitted to retain the sweating bag of very gooey butter which a police officer snatched from my hand and dumped in a bin. That was the end of my Da's buttered spuds and, more importantly, the distinct possibility of a good hiding from Cassie Ann.

Several hours passed before a tired-looking young constable appeared and slowly opened the cell door. Bit of a surprise really as we thought that a night in the cells was a given and we had resigned ourselves to the discomfort and, of course, the notoriety. The young constable beckoned me to follow him to the front desk and there she was, Cassie Ann, wearing a full-length raincoat that she had bought at a jumble sale and had seen better days, holding a short umbrella in her right hand and with a face like thunder. She did not hit me, at first. In front of a hesitant-looking Desk Sergeant and the young constable, Cassie Ann threatened to do all sorts to me for embarrassing her in front of these decent Protestant policemen, one of whom very quickly reached for the handle on the front door, held it open and gently ushered me and my mother out into the street.

It was not the arrest that really annoyed her you see; it was the butter, or lack of it, for my father's spuds. With the sun splitting the stones and her wrapped in her raincoat Cassie Ann made a great effort to chase me all the way home whilst waving her umbrella in my general direction. I could run but I certainly could not hide from her wrath. Daddy was not that fussed though. He thought the episode was quite funny although he dare not laugh when Cassie Ann was in the room. Not that he was frightened of her, rather he was just a bit reluctant to argue with Cassie Ann. It was to be several days of complete silence and the avoidance from her before the thaw eventually broke.

"If you want butter for your spuds with your dinner, you'll have to go the co-op and pay for it out of your own money, if you have any." There was a hint of a smile on her face when she said those first words to me in the kitchen a few days later. You could never stop loving that woman.

But never again was I requested to go shopping for a pound of butter for the father's spuds especially when there was a possibility of a bit of bother with the local constabulary in the town.

Orangemen and Marches

The Loyal Orange Institution, commonly known as 'the Orange Order', is a Protestant fraternal society in Northern Ireland. The Order was founded in 1790 in County Armagh during a violent period of sectarian conflict between Protestants and Catholics where its principal objective was to maintain the Protestant Ascendancy. As a strict Protestant society, it does not accept non-protestants into its ranks as members, unless they convert and adhere to the principles of the Order and most certainly there is no tolerance for Protestants marrying Catholics. Every year, many of its lodges across Northern Ireland arrange marches where well-drilled bandsmen parade through most towns and villages irrespective of whether much of the population is Catholic or Protestant.

Growing up in a Catholic environment and with very limited access to the 'other side', we just accepted that Orangemen had the divine right to march behind their bands and massive banners showing a hunchbacked, King William of Holland on a white horse, defeating King James of Scotland at a battle near the River Boyne in deepest Ireland on 12th July 1690. Historically, the battle took place on the 1st of July, but Pope Gregory and his Gregorian calendar changed the dates although some Orangemen had no time for that man in Rome and just ignored the change and refused to recognise that the world had moved on. As teenagers, we were happy to stand on the sidewalk and watch these colourful bands wearing formal military-style uniforms as the marched past us playing tunes that were more melodic than offensive. Members of the Order, including the Grandmaster, would march in strict formation behind the bands, wearing bowler hats and orange sashes around their necks with the insignia LOL on them, meaning 'Loyal Orange Lodge', the number indicating the local lodge to which they belonged. The repertoire of the music and the musicality were usually excellent and even enjoyable to listen to and whistle along with. There was seldom any trouble other than some drunk shouting incoherent abuse at the bands. As the years went by and the civil unrest spread amongst both communities, the marches took on a more sinister and aggressive style. They were no longer welcome in many Catholic areas and fighting would usually lead to rioting, and invariably the outcome was violence and mayhem.

Felix used to work with numerous Protestants when he collected pigs from local farms and take them to the abattoir for slaughter. The majority of the farmers were of good Protestant stock and Felix, a man who had lived in America and was a mild-mannered individual who did not judge people by their religion nor their political leanings, he always looked for the good in them, was close friends with many Protestants. In order to commemorate the Battle of the Boyne, every 12th July was deemed as a public holiday thereby permitting the Orangemen to parade behind their bands and to eventually rest their weary legs at the end of a long sweltering day in some field listening to endless sermons from some obscure cleric. One gloriously sunny day, several Orangemen, who were friends of Felix, met him in Friel's Pub for a few pints of Guinness and the occasional Powers whiskey before taking their rightful place behind their lodge band that would soon be marching through the town.

The first we knew that there was a problem was when a very distressed Mrs Quinn appeared in the kitchen of our house and declared that she had just witnessed something that would take Cassie's very breath away. Felix, wearing an Orange Sash, was spotted marching behind a Loyal Sons of Ulster Pipe Band, smiling and waving to the crowds gathered on the pavements to cheer on the Brethren. Cassie near fainted. She sat heavily on a small chair beside the kitchen table, holding her multi-stained apron to her mouth and uttered:

"Oh, Sweet Jesus, what is to become of us this day."

Mrs Quinn extracted a tiny white handkerchief from her coat pocket and after wiping the sweat from her own top lip, handed it to Cassie Ann who loudly blew her nose into Mrs Quinn's delicate little handkerchief.

"Orangemen. He is walking with Orangemen and him a good Catholic. Jesus, the shame. How am I to live with the shame. That man of mine in the Orange Order. I'll kill that father of yours when I lay my hands on him," she screamed as she looked around at us young ones, our mouths wide open but with just a hint of a smile on them.

"You two, get out there and bring that drunken disgrace of a man home with you," as she pointed at my older brother and me. "How on God's good earth am I to face those ones at Bingo on Friday night. I will take the head of him when I get my hands on him, the traitor. And be quick about it. Do you hear me you wee skitters?" She shouted at us as we headed towards the front door not daring to glance back at a very angry Cassie Ann.

We followed the sounds of the bands that echoed from the centre of the town. Some bands had enormous instruments called Lambeg Drums made from goat skins with which they would beat continuously with curved Malacca canes to make a sound that was difficult to comprehend as music. The Lambeg Drum weighs approximately 40lbs and is carried by strong young men, using a harness hung from their thick necks to retain the instrument whilst it is being played. Giving a sound of over 120 decibels, it is one of the world's loudest acoustic instruments.

It was in that general direction that we set off in search of Felix, the recently adopted and now fully-fledged Orangeman, albeit only temporarily. A few minutes after arriving in the middle of the town and wheedling our way amongst the large crowd of followers who were thoroughly enjoying the annual festival of marching and drum banging, we spotted him. There he was walking in the centre of a group of bowler-hatted men, three abreast alongside two of his pals from work whom we recognised. He was wearing an 'Orange Sash' with some lodge number attached to it but thankfully; there was no bowler hat upon his head. Instead, he wore the Sunday hat, the good one that he wore to Mass. He looked so happy and content and was even marching in step with his pals behind the pipe band whose musicians wore tartan kilts and woollen Glengarry bonnets on their heads.

It was then he spotted the two of us. He waved, his lopsided drunken smile widening as he nudged the other two marchers to look in our general direction. We could almost make out his mouthing the words "that's my two boys over there," and then his friends started waving and we returned their gesture. For all intents, we were two young Protestant lads waving at a family member who was having a lovely day marching behind a band with his best friends on the Glorious 12th of July. There was nothing for it but to follow the parade until it arrived at the field, a mile or so outside the town where the band members and their followers would rest and listen to the interminable speeches about God, the Queen and her beloved country. Eventually, we collared Felix and he gave each of us a pat on the back. We quietly suggested that we all go home together. He had other ideas. Still wearing their sashes, his pals joined us and recommended, with considerable conviction, that they all go for one final drink, just the one, in a pub at the bottom of the town. Felix slipped each of us some loose change and waved us off with a gentle warning:

"Tell your mother that you never saw me. I will be back in a wee while and not to worry. Off you go now boys and say nothing."

It was after 10 pm when he staggered through the front door. Cassie Ann was sitting in the kitchen with our permanent lodger, Kirk from Dunkirk.

"Would you look at the state of that one there, Johnny Kirk?" who nodded in agreement, although he had the wit to never disagree with Cassie Ann on any subject.

"Am I right or wrong Johnny?" she would frequently shout in his direction thinking he was deaf, which he wasn't, and he would always nod his ascent.

"Look at him, would you. For the life of Jesus, what is to become of us. And him, as drunk as a skunk and stinking to the high heavens. Ashamed you should be, do you hear me? Ashamed!" We three boys just sat on the battered settee and watched as the one-sided row developed with Cassie Ann, her face becoming even more redder in the face as the anger rose within her. Felix simply stood up straight from the kitchen chair where he had parked his arse, removed his Sunday hat from his head and with great nonchalance and a grin on his face, threw it in the general direction of a large nail hanging from the back of the kitchen door. He missed. He burped, smiled broadly, and with a wave of his right hand, he turned on his heels and headed for the stairs. A dignified retreat in the face of overwhelming opposition. Of course, it was many months afterwards before we heard the last of his one and only adventure with a band of Orangemen. And it was to be a very long time before Felix was granted permission by Cassie Ann to enjoy a drink again in any public house in that little town.

Many years later and long after Cassie Ann passed away, over a glass of Guinness in Friel's he confided in me about that day when he was seen marching with those Orangemen.

"One of the best days craic I ever had in this buck mad country of ours. You know, Son, I might just have made a really good Orangeman if it wasn't for me being a Catholic." I couldn't have agreed more with Felix. I could just envisage hm enjoying the music and marching behind the bands with his Protestant friends. The man certainly had rhythm.

Life for teenagers across Northern Ireland was becoming increasingly dangerous. Listening to the nightly news bulletins and watching the tragic outcomes of huge car bombs and the murder of so many on either side of the divide it was inevitable that so many young people from both religious persuasions were being dragged into the bitter conflict.

Meeting up with friends during the dark autumn evenings was fraught with danger. The inevitable stop and search by British soldiers, their faces streaked dark with camouflage paint, was a regular occurrence. These were just young men from the North of England who had joined the army as an escape from unemployment and were now patrolling streets where they felt unwelcome and would rather be elsewhere. In this part of their UK, they were never made welcome especially in our beleaguered little town. Being stopped by the 'B' Specials was an altogether different prospect. This was a reserve police force, drawn mostly from the farming community all of whom were of the Protestant faith. Also known as B Men, they were a quasi-military reserve police force, set up many years shortly before the partition of Ireland. The B Men would be used to set-up roadblocks and annoy anyone with a Christian name that sounded remotely Catholic and to support the regular RUC officers when there was rioting, especially in Catholic areas. Heavy-handed was one of the few ways to describe these farmers with weapons and ammunitions in abundance. They took immense pleasure and a certain amount of pride in dolling out a good hiding to any Catholics, young or old, who had the temerity to challenge them or to fail to answer their questions. An encounter with these uniformed thugs was to be avoided at all costs.

Their official title was 'The Ulster Special Constabulary' of which there were some 20,000 operational during the conflict. They were notorious for their participation in quelling riots frequently with the use of lethal force. In 1969, the Specials, who had absolutely nothing to do with an Indie band from the English West Midlands, shot and wounded a number of people in various towns and rural communities across Tyrone and Derry. This resulted in an investigation conducted by a British judge, Lord Scarman, whose findings were 'that they were at a loss to find any rational explanation for the fatal shooting and wounding of so many innocent people'. The tribunal's findings determined that the Specials were reckless and irresponsible. These men, in their black heavy oil skin raincoats and ill-fighting helmets, would torment and aggravate young men to the extent that any response, either verbal or physical, would inevitably result in a slap on the mouth with the butt of a fully loaded Lee Enfield rifle.

Following numerous well publicised incidents of brutal attacks in many Catholic areas the consequences of which resulted in huge embarrassment for the British Government of the day, the Specials were disbanded in 1969 and replaced with the Ulster Defence Regiment, a reserve British Army force. The

Specials immediately joined the new force en masse, and those that could not be bothered were permitted to retain their weapons for personal use. In effect, the same well-armed Loyalist outfit continued their brutal behaviour but now wearing a different uniform, one that made them appear to members of the British Army. *Plus, ca change plus ca meme bloody army* as the French might call it!

The UDR, as they were known shortly after their formation, was a Protestant force but with initially up to 18% Catholic representation although this figure quickly dropped back to 2% following intimidation from Republicans. The first fatality in the regiment was a Catholic who was murdered when he was at home with his wife and five children. The IRA claimed responsibility for the killing that immediately sent out a clear message to all other Catholic members of the regiment that they too would be a target if they remained in the UDR. Following the murder, forty Catholics resigned from the regiment. The UDR was an infantry regiment of the British Army and therefore subject to all their regulations and controls but, in practice, the regiment had little regard for the rights of the nationalist people and openly demonstrated this on numerous occasions.

It was against this backdrop of militarism and brutality that young teenage lads tried to have a life outside the constant bombardment of news of atrocities committed by both sides and the daily risk of being searched, intimidated and physically abused. When stopped late at night by a UDR patrol, groups of young men would be lined up against a nearby wall and aggressively searched for whatever the soldiers deemed as weapons. This meant that none of us would dare risk carrying a penknife or even a sharp pencil as such might be deemed as offensive weapons and invariably attract a good kicking. Was it any wonder, therefore, that the IRA, for its many faults, seemed such an attractive proposition to young Catholic men who had endured enough of the regular intimidation and brutality from the British Army.

Aunties

Cassie Ann's last remaining aunt died at the age of 94, alone on her farm in remote County Fermanagh. My mother had an expectation that as the only remaining relative, the farm would be left to her. It did not happen. I was home for a short break from London when the news of her aunt's death filtered through to Cassie Ann and arrangements were made to visit her remains. She insisted on taking me to Alice's Wake for support. We set out for the Wake on the evening before the funeral and we made our way to the farm and joined the other mourners in celebrating the life of the aged aunt.

The neighbours had made all the necessary arrangements including the food and drink and even had cigarettes laid out on saucers for the attendees of the Wake. After the initial introduction and expressions of condolences, we sat down with the owners of next door's farm. It was shortly into the conversation that Cassie Ann was informed that the very farm that she had high hopes of obtaining in the Will had now been left to a near neighbour instead. In fact, the very people now commiserating with us on our sad loss. Upon realising that she was not to be the beneficiary of the farm, Cassie Ann promptly rose to her feet, grabbed me by the left shoulder and pulled me over to the side of the coffin.

"You were nothing but a tight auld bitch of a woman all your life," she shouted close to the right ear of the wizened corpse in the coffin. "I have come to your Wake only because I am a good Catholic; but if my veins weren't so bad, I would jump on your grave."

A priest approached Cassie Ann and asked if there was anything he could do or say to help alleviate her grief.

"Don't be sticking your priestly nose where it doesn't belong and out of my way before I lay a hand on you, Father." I tried not to laugh but she saw me and scowled and then proceeded to pull me out of the house, into the car parked nearby and off we went. There was very little conversation on the way home but, for once, I think I heard a few expletives.

The heavens had quite literally opened when we returned for the funeral and internment the following morning. The church was a cold and very bleak building with a sparse congregation who were mostly in their upper 70s and 80s. At Cassie Ann's insistence, we sat near the rear of the church ensuring that we were as far away from the front pews where the mourners were seated and certainly out of sight of the beneficiaries of the Will. I never really knew Alice and the only memory that I had of my great aunt was when as very young child being taken to meet her and her husband on their remote farm. I still recalled seeing her for the very first time and the fear she instilled in me with her abrupt manner and her gaunt appearance. She had hair streaked through with grey which was tied in a tight bun near the top of her head. Aunt Alice was not a friendly relative. Nor a particularly generous one as we were to find out.

Aunt Mary was my father's only surviving sister. His only other sister, Theresa, had died at the age of 16 during the great influenza pandemic of 1918-1919 that killed more people in Europe than in the Great War. It was also known as the Spanish Flu and somewhere between 20 and 40 million died with estimates at the time of over a fifth of the world's population having been infected. Mary married late in life. A bachelor farmer who lived near Lower Lock Erne in remote County Fermanagh, was attracted to Mary at a Fair Day where cattle and sheep were being auctioned. The two of them were a perfect match, both being gentle people and good-humoured. They enjoyed entertaining the neighbouring farmers in their home that was situated close to a hidden beauty spot through which a tributary flowed into Lough Erne. It was known locally as Drummoney Falls, a place where we played as youngsters and its beauty is forever etched on our souls. In her 40s Mary gave birth to a baby boy but the child did not survive beyond his first birthday and, sadly, there were to be no other births thereafter.

Mary's husband died of cancer when she was in her early 60s. However, she remained on the farm for many years until her eyesight began to fail and carefully managed the letting of the hundred-acre farm to neighbours who would rent the fields from her in order to graze their cattle on the less boggy parts and to grow hay for silage to feed the animals during the harsh winters. Every evening a steady stream of friends and neighbours would dander up the road to Mary's house to enjoy a chat over a cup of tea and the occasional biscuit. There were no barriers to those who wished to pop in of an evening where the assembled cast would discuss the price of cattle and sheep sold at recent auctions or to just catch up on gossip especially news about who had died or who might be in pursuit of a husband or a wife. Protestants and Catholics mixed happily together without resorting to any talk about religion or politics.

Mary, wearing her extra-strong NHS spectacles, would sit in her armchair beside the cream-coloured range that was used both for cooking and for heating and listen intently all evening to the ramblings of her visitors. The house was a two-storey building with three small bedrooms upstairs and kitchen and sitting room downstairs. The sitting room, more commonly known as the front room, was only used on special occasions such as when the local priest or doctor were doing their rounds or when there were visitors from afar. There was an ancient organ in the corner of the front room which one was played by one of her nightly visitors, a man of the Methodist persuasion, who would entertain the audience to several renditions of a selection of hymns. But as the instrument had not been tuned for many years, the sound that emanated from it was not great and the hymns indistinguishable as the merged into each other. Nonetheless, the little Protestant man, made every effort to wring a few passable notes out of the instrument with which to accompany his out-of-key rendition of How Great Thou Art, the one hymn which he knew the words of in its entirety.

In the tiny hall or vestibule at the entrance to the kitchen, stood a white enamel bucket filled with fresh water that would be drawn by hand each day from a nearby small spring well. There was no indoor bathroom nor toilet and the only water supply that was available was from the well. Whether in the dark freezing cold of winter or during the wet days of spring and autumn, the water bucket would require filling each day and evening in order that the residents of the house could wash themselves and make their hot drinks. As for the lavatory, there was a dry toilet at the back of the house where those using it would sit or squat over a wooden seat to do their business into a very deep hole after which some lime would be poured. The one benefit of that toilet was that it had a pedestal of sorts, so your arse didn't get trapped in the hole if you had a bit too much alcohol the night before. In the event that it was a merely a pish that was required there were acres of trees surrounding the house and it was simply a case of finding a suitable one nearby.

Mary once had an interesting confrontation with the British Army. In her defence, she was not aware that it was the army but in her very own words the story is as follows:

"A large contraption of a machine landed in my front field the other day and scared the cows, who took to their hooves and scarpered. A crowd of peculiar-sounding men wearing strange outfits and carrying guns, ran out of the machine and hid behind bushes. Two of them then came up to the front door and knocked loudly on it. Maisie was in the house with me at the time, helping to clean the place. She answered the door and asked what they wanted. But they pushed past the poor woman without as much as a by your leave and started looking in all the rooms and searching through drawers and under beds. When they were finished ransacking the house, the manager of the army, a nice man with lovely clean skin and nice nails, spoke to me in a language that I just could not understand a word but Maisie said she could as she was a Protestant. She told me that he was a captain or general or something in the army and they were looking for terrorists as there was a rumour that they were plenty of them hiding around here. I told Maisie to tell him that we don't put up with that sort of nonsense in these parts and he just seemed to wipe his forehead but Maisie said that he had actually saluted. She has a brother in the Ulster Defence Regiment and knows about those things. And then, the manager or captain or whatever he called himself turned his back on me and scampered back to the big noisy machine and off it flew into the clouds. We never saw the likes of him or that machine of his ever again, thanks be to God."

Mary had always been a countrywoman and never travelled far from home other than to the markets, or the occasional day trip to the beach in County Donegal in the nearby Irish Republic. When she told me this story, I tried to feel what she must have imagined when witnessing a Wessex or Chinook Helicopter, landing in front of her house and camouflaged soldiers carrying automatic rifles scurrying about must have looked through her eyes. Mary had never seen an aeroplane, never mind a troop-carrying helicopter. And the posh voice of a British army officer, who probably attended Eton and Sandhurst, must have perplexed and frightened the old lady but the army had a job to do and unfortunately, compassion was never one of their strong points.

Close to where Mary lived was the small town of Pettigo where she would visit once a week for her grocery shopping. It is a small village straddling the border of County Fermanagh in Northern Ireland and County Donegal in the Irish Republic. Once a thriving market village, it suffered from partition in 1921 when the six counties in the North were retained under the jurisdiction of the United Kingdom and the other 26 counties became the Irish Republic. During the height of the Troubles numerous cross-border roads such as Pettigo and other small towns straddling the two parts of the now divided country had checkpoints erected by the British Army and the UDR under the pretence of looking for terrorists. This had the effect of cutting Pettigo off from much of its rural hinterland in counties Fermanagh and Tyrone. The little hamlet was split down the middle by a heavily fortified barrier of sandbags and gun emplacements that required motorists to stop and be subjected to rigorous searches and the occasional interrogation by young British soldiers. Local residents had to navigate this impediment several times each day whether coming or going to their place of work or attending their respective churches. Pettigo was a microcosm of what Northern Ireland would become during the Troubles.

At the age of 67, Mary decided that she would like to try smoking cigarettes. Every evening she would sit in her armchair in the corner of the kitchen gazing at her visitors as they smoked endless cigarettes and flicking their ash on to the slab flooring of her kitchen. Farmers, in long wellington boots, with bits of dried cow dung stuck to their soles and others wearing hob-nailed shoes that were perfect for walking over rough terrain, would sit around most of the evening in Mary's house drinking tea and belching whilst gossiping and smoking.

Mary enjoyed her first cigarette so much that she decided to start smoking full-time. Maisie would buy her 20 Players Navy Cut every other day and Mary would sit with her neighbours during the evening visits and chat and smoke with great gusto. Players were the most popular brand across the UK with up to two-thirds of all cigarettes being sold to consumers and cancer victims. They were the preferred smoke for the bachelor farmers who spent their evenings with Mary. Mind you there was a marked difference between Mary and the other smokers. Mary did not inhale. It was simply a case of lots of puffing, and because her eyesight was failing, she never quite knew when to flick the ever-expanding ash on the end of her fag which would occasionally end up in the cup of tea on the table beside her chair. She still drank the tea, ash or no ash.

Mary eventually moved from her remote farm in Fermanagh into our house on the Derry Road to spend the rest of her days with Felix. Cassie Ann had recently died and as Mary's eyesight was failing and Felix had lost his wife, it was the most pragmatic solution for them both. There was a constant stream of visitors to the house, so Mary instantly felt at home as she would listen to the chat and gossip whilst seated beside the open fire in the warm and cosy kitchen smoking a cigarette and enjoying a cup of tea.

Felix also had a permanent lodger living with them who went by the name of Jackie Boyle. Jackie had recently retired as a cleaner at the local Post Office and had come to live with us when Cassie Ann was alive. He had a fondness for alcohol but, unfortunately, that fondness was not reciprocated. Jackie, whose catchphrase was 'See Me' would become uproariously drunk on those days after he received both his State and Post Office pension. But first he would ensure that the house on the Derry Road was thoroughly cleansed each morning, the open fire in the kitchen cleared of ashes and debris and made sure that the colony of cats and scabby dogs were well-fed before making his way to the bookies in Castle Street. His early routine entailed checking the day's runners and riders in that morning's edition of the Daily Mirror that Felix had purchased on his way home from 10 am Mass in the Sacred Heart Church. Having wagered his bets on the absolute 'good things' or 'certainties' for that afternoon's racing in Curley's bookies, he would adjourn to Friel's pub where he and others without gainful employment, would drink, smoke and listen out for the results of that day's racing from Kempton Park or Sandown on the radio. Jackie was a small man with a very large and generous heart and an even bigger smile that contained a full set of false teeth. He was a great raconteur who would drink to excess, especially if one of the selections made it past the winning post in the first place, which was rare, and after buying drinks for everyone, he would inevitably collapse in a heap in one of the chairs in the public bar of Friel's Pub.

Felix, who was a part-time lollipop man, was conveniently stationed at a road crossing directly opposite Friel's Bar. When he finished his afternoon shift of escorting unruly children from the local primary school over the busy road, he would pop into the bar to join Jackie and wet his lips with a bottle of Guinness or two. Having helped weans across the road it was then Felix's duty to extract the sometimes comatose and often heavily intoxicated Jackie from Friel's Pub and escort him the short distance up the hill towards the house on the Derry Road, some 300 yards away. If Jackie struggled to walk or stagger up the hill Felix, a strong man even in his 70s, would lift tiny Jackie on to his shoulders and casually walk home with a very drunk lodger on his back. The neighbours would not look twice at this regular occurrence.

Life for Jackie in his early days was not a pleasant one. He was born into a large dysfunctional Protestant family in a small village near to the town. At the age of 17, he joined the Royal Enniskillen Fusiliers in the late 1930s and eventually saw action in Europe during the Second World War. In January 1944, Jackie was part of the Allied landings in Italy under the leadership of General Harold Alexander, the commander of the First Infantry Brigade. The battalion that Jackie served in was attempting to overrun the Germans who were embedded at the top of Monte Cassino, a mountainous terrain where the historic abbey dominated the nearby towns of Cassino and the entrances to the Liri and Rapido valleys. Because of its strategic importance, it was heavily defended by the German forces who pinned down the Allies on the steep slopes below Cassino during the long and very harsh Italian winter months. The Abbey, which was erected in AD 529, was being used by the German occupiers as an observation point. The building, and most of its unwanted occupants, was eventually destroyed by American bombers who dropped 1,400 tons of high explosives on to the location. The cost to the Allied forces was 55,000 casualties with far fewer on the German side, estimated at 20,000 dead. In the midst of all this mayhem was Jackie Boyle, a gregarious little man from the back end of Tyrone who spent many freezing days and nights under constant bombardment in a strange land where the stress of the battle eventually took its toll on his mind and body. In the end, his nerves shattered, he was removed from the hills around Cassino and hospitalised. His war was over. It was hardly surprising that Jackie took to the drink in later years.

A heavy smoker and equally heavy drinker, his blood circulation was poor and it took several hours of rubbing his legs to get them moving each morning. He was looking forward to meeting up with his estranged family and had bought presents for his brother and his wife. He had travelled by bus to his brother's house in a neighbouring village, looking particularly dapper in the new suit bought for him by my younger brother. On Boxing Day, Felix received the fateful phone call from Jackie's sister-in-law to inform him that he had succumbed to a heart attack a few hours earlier. As the local doctor had signed the death certificate stating that it was indeed a fatal heart attack, it was decided by his family that he would be waked in his brother's house in the village and subsequently laid to rest in the Protestant cemetery following the funeral service in the local Church of Ireland. Not that Jackie was religious in the slightest, but death is a great reconciler to religion even if not requested. On the day of the funeral, it seemed that everyone in the town whoever had a drink with Jackie or had any conversation with him or even had the privilege of helping to carry him home to his lodgings attended the funeral. Catholics, Protestants and Dissenters converged on the village and duly observed the rituals of the service in the Protestant Church and prayed for the repose of the soul of a dear little man who touched so many lives. Felix was overcome at the suddenness of his passing and would miss his friend, lodger and occasional drinking partner.

Drink flowed all that afternoon in the closest pub to the cemetery and it was only at closing time that the soberest amongst the happy mourners took charge of the keys to the numerous vehicles and drove those who were fit to stand to their respective homes. Jackie had a wondrous and truly memorable send-off and one for fit for a hero, the unsung Hero of Monte Cassino.

From Brook Street to Old Broad Street

It was a time of riots and rampant violence throughout the province. Each new day brought news of yet more bombings and killings so much so that it became the norm. Bands avoided coming to the country and only the local showbands would chance driving around the rural halls to play music to the entertainment-starved teenagers. One such group was the Miami Showband from the Irish Republic. They were the most popular, crowd-pleasing showband in Ireland and had enormous success having notched up seven number one records in the Irish singles charts during the 1960s and 1970s. The band was led by one of the country's most high-profile singers, Dickie Rock, and later by Fran O'Toole. In 1975, band members Fran O'Toole, Tony Geraghty and Brian McCoy were murdered when the minibus in which they were travelling home from a gig in County Down in Northern Ireland was stopped at a bogus military checkpoint by gunmen dressed in British Army uniforms. All the band members were ordered to get out of the minibus and were lined up by the roadside waiting to be searched and questioned. It subsequently transpired that the gunmen were members of an extreme loyalist paramilitary group, the Ulster Volunteer Force. Whilst several of the ambushers stood guard over the band members, two of the gunmen endeavoured to hide a time bomb in the minibus but it exploded prematurely killing the perpetrators instantly. The remaining gunmen then opened fire on the band members killing O'Toole, McCoy and Geraghty and wounding Lee and Travers, both of whom ran across fields to escape with blood pouring from their wounds. The murder of these icons of the music world created a sense of outrage amongst the Nationalist and Protestant communities. Sadly, it also spread fear in the community with parents being very reluctant to allow their teenage children to meet at venues where further atrocities might occur. Life after the massacre of the Miami Showband took on an altogether different complexion.

Touring showbands were exclusively an Irish invention. Ballrooms of romance, as some were known due to the likelihood of meeting someone from the opposite sex without the supervision of nosey priests, were commonplace in rural communities. These makeshift meeting halls were located in villages and towns across the length and breadth of Ireland and when a well-known band was playing, young people would don their finest clothes and flock to the venues in their hundreds. Starved of entertainment and fed up with the constant news of murder and mayhem across the country, young people would seek out those ballrooms where showbands would be appearing, even if it was in a marquee or simply a large tent located in the back of beyond. Farmers' sons would drive their father's tractors to the venue and if it had a trailer, it was not unusual to catch sight of it loaded with lads and girls being driving home along the dark roads of the countryside. Of course, there would be the wannabee terrorists who would send a message to the local police station or, more often the Parish Priest, indicating that a bomb had been planted in or near to some venue where the dance was to take place. Teenagers followed local bands such as The Undertones from Derry and Belfast's Stiff Little Fingers, both popular punk rock groups and very much anti-establishment, which was hardly surprising as the Government of the day was headless and close to the point of collapse.

For most teenagers of the period, it was both a fascinating and a very frightening time to be growing up in the North of Ireland. But occasionally a hero or a heroine would appear from relative obscurity and would offer a glimmer of hope for the future of the country. One such person was a young and very engaging Bernadette Devlin. She had been studying at Queen's University in Belfast and stood for the UK Parliament in the seat known as Mid Ulster. She was elected to a backdrop of bitter sectarianism, but she had the strength of character and determination to rise above the bigotry and made her way to the Palace of Westminster as the youngest ever elected female MP. She became an instant hero when she slapped the Home Secretary, Reginald Maudling, across the face during a debate about the Troubles in the House of Commons. Years later, Bernadette and her husband were shot by members of the Ulster Freedom Fighters, who broke into their home and shot her nine times in front of her children. British soldiers were watching the family home at the time but failed to prevent the assassination attempt. We youngsters loved everything about Bernadette. Her strident passion, her brazen cheek in take on the establishment, her desire for equality for all and even her kinky long boots. We were only 16 or 17 so we could dream. With Bernadette as our MP, we had high hopes of many changes that would deliver justice to the Nationalist people but, instead, there was a rapid descent into chaos and unrelenting violence. The Six Counties that made up Northern Ireland was now even more divided with each side becoming more entrenched in their hatred for each other. Life was no longer an adventure but one of fear and trepidation every time we stepped out the front door.

Having left the confines of the Christian Brothers, my mother suggested that I move to England and see if I could make something of my life. The options for staying put were limited, the likelihood of a decent job was next to nil, an early death or imprisonment was a distinct possibility. She was right, of course. There was no future staying in that little town and without argument I agreed with her and decided that I would take Cassie Ann's advice and try my luck in London. It couldn't be any worse that remaining at home waiting for the next riot or bomb to go off in the middle of the town. A friend suggested that the Dole Office might help with the fare as I would be saving them money by not being on their books of the many unemployed Catholics. I sought a meeting with them to announce that I was off on a big adventure and that I required a bit of funding. At the appointed hour, I arrived for so-called 'exit interview' with the man at the Dole Office who was responsible for my departure. He was a pleasant individual called George and happy to provide me with a ticket for the ferry to Holyhead and then a rail ticket to London. He seemed really pleased with my request and I was grateful to him for his kindness. Looking at the ticket, I noticed that it was one-way only, so I asked if I could have a return one as I might change my mind if I didn't like the place. He smiled. Then, he slowly shook his head, rose to his feet and opened the door to show me the way out and not another word was said. There was to be no returning home for yet another youngster from the wrong side of the religious divide.

On the day of the departure from my home to the exciting big city of London, a place I could only dream of, Cassie Ann stood in the doorway of our house on the Derry Road and offered her hand to me to shake. We are not a tactile people and handshakes amongst close family members were about the extent of any physical contact even if it was your mother. Being the big softy that I was, my overriding desire was to wrap my arms around her and hold her close for a few seconds. But Cassie Ann would have been too embarrassed. She put her hand out and I shook it but held it for a few seconds and then turned to walk up the street to meet a friend who had arranged a lift to Belfast Harbour and the ferry to Holyhead. I turned to wave and saw that she had something in her hands and she beckoned me to return. She presented me with a small bottle of Holy Water from the Basilica at Knock in the West of Ireland. She instructed me to bless myself with the Holy Water every morning and every night so as to ward of the evils of dirty women and Protestants. As I slowly ambled away from her, she shouted after me, "God love and protect you son. And do not forget what I said about those dirty English women. You keep your distance from them that's a good cub." I waved back at her as she put her stain-covered apron to her lips, but inside I was just desperate to find any woman, dirty or not and even an English one would do. I bounced up that road with a broad smile on my face.

I had just turned 20 when I arrived alone at Euston Station on a cold Winter's morning with my battered tiny suitcase held together with an ancient belt that I had borrowed from Felix. Cassie Ann, not exactly the most travelled of people although, she had once visited Belfast on a day trip when the trains were running, had warned me to hide all my money in my socks in case I was robbed. The few pound notes that I did possess were safely tucked inside my right sock before I left home. When I eventually figured out the London Underground map, I found myself standing on the platform at Euston Underground Station waiting for a tube train. It was astonishing to witness the speed of the train as it sped out of the dark tunnel and abruptly halted to allow passengers to disembark on to the platforms allowing other passengers to enter the carriages. I allowed three trains to pass before I struck up the courage to jump into one of the carriages. For the life of me I could not understand how people were not squashed to death every day by those sliding doors. It was only later that I realised there was a guard in the end carriage who worked the doors and could see the entire platform.

My pre-arranged accommodation in London was to share a room in a hostel near Notting Hill Underground station, only for a few nights with five other lads who came from various parts of England. These lads were friendly and chatty but they had great difficulty understanding my accent and, in return, I just used to guess what they were chatting about. After days of trawling around London, looking for a job, I returned to the hostel one evening and discovered that most of my belongings had disappeared along with all the other lads and none of the staff knew anything. I gathered up what was left of my belongings and took myself off to find a pub in North London that my older brother had worked in. The pub was called the Cock Tavern located in Palmers Green, an outer suburb of the city. It was late afternoon when I arrived at the backdoor and was met by the Landlady's mother, a delightful English woman in her late 70s. After enquiring what I was after, she invited me into the kitchen and taking one look at the bedraggled state of me, she decided that I needed something substantial to eat. She sat me down at a large table in the cavernous kitchen and promptly took an enormous frying pan from a drawer, greased it and slapped four or five pieces of bacon on it followed by three eggs and a sliced tomato. The plate of food she presented to me with was rapidly smothered with Heinz Brown Sauce and greedily devoured in just a few minutes.

"You were hungry then, Son," she said in a broad cockney accent.

"Thank you Mrs. I really was hungry and appreciate what you just did for me," I replied looking ashamed of myself for having put her to all that bother.

"Right then, young man, my daughter and that husband of hers run this pub and they are looking for an apprentice cellarman; and I believe that you fit the bill perfectly," she announced and with that, she went to the door leading to their living quarters and shouted for her daughter to come to the kitchen right away.

"I've found your new cellarman, Annie," she bellowed up the stairs.

The landlady, a curvaceously attractive-looking woman in her late 40s, appeared at the door. She was smoking a cigarette inserted in a long black holder, not unlike the one that Marlene Dietrich smoked in the film *Touch of Evil*, a film that my friends and I had wormed our way into the County Cinema to watch many years earlier.

"Well, let's have a look at this new man then," she replied as she walked towards me. I had now stood up from the table and was desperately trying to stick my chest out and praying that my face wouldn't turn bright red.

"You look very young but very cute my young man. Well, if Mother here thinks you will do, then so be it. Have you anywhere to live? You look a bit lost, to be honest," she said in a soft croaky voice that had obviously endured far too many cigarettes over the years.

"I live in a hostel in Notting Hill, but it's not great though," I replied in a barely audible voice.

"Right, then you go and fetch your things and bring them here this evening, and you can share a room with that Aussie fellow, Barry. He'll look after you until you find your feet here."

And that fortuitous meeting with Mrs B and her mother was to be the start of a long and fruitful relationship with the Cock Tavern and its strange and exotic inhabitants in glorious North London.

The following morning after having the first decent night's sleep in ages, I was put to work as a live-in cellarman. The majority of my time was spent in the depths of the pub, learning out to clean and flush beer lines thus ensuring that the three bars received a constant flow of beers, most of which I had never heard of. Ken, the Landlord, whom I met first thing over breakfast, was a middle-aged man with a fondness for the opposite sex even though he was supposedly married to Annie, my boss and the Landlady. He was a heavy smoker and enjoyed a large gin and tonic as soon as opening time came around. He was pleasant to me and even tolerated it when I would send the wrong beer to one of the pumps in the three bars. Michael, an Irishman from Sligo, who had one leg shorter than the other, was the bar manager and an even-tempered man with an outrageous sense of humour. It was he who guided me on all things to do with bar work and, occasionally, he would take me into the main lounge and show me how to pour the bottled beers and how to mix drinks without making a fool of myself and annoying the customers. Michael was also a consummate smoker along with Steve, the other permanent bar staff and, for a while, I was convinced that it was compulsory for all staff to smoke in pubs in London. In the public bar, where there was no dress code for the customers, the clientele was all Irish navvies with a sprinkling of Jamaican lads and a couple of Glaswegians. This bar was the liveliest and most entertaining of the three, especially at closing time on a Saturday evening when the effects of a day's drinking of countless pints of Guinness invariably resulted in arguments and the occasional punch-up that would be swiftly resolved by a hardnosed bouncer from the Gorbals. None of the Irish lads could understand a single word he said but when his fists were flying, they got the message.

Every Wednesday evening and Sunday mornings, Ken the Governor or Gov, as he liked to be addressed, would promote strip shows in the vast saloon bar. These two days were the highlight of the week and real money spinners for Ken. The audience was all male many of whom would queue at the main entrance long before opening time in order to grab the seats nearest the tiny stage. I was always working in the cellar when the performances were underway but I was aware of the clapping, cheering and the loud music belting out from the bar above. I also took a peep every now and then when then artistes were in full flow. One Sunday morning, after only a few weeks into the job, Ken summoned me from the cellar and announced that the Gorbals bouncer had been arrested for grievous bodily harm during some altercation in Wood Green the night before and, as a consequence, a replacement was required to escort the artistes to the stage.

"But Governor please I would not have a clue what to do, honestly. I would be a real embarrassment." I replied sheepishly.

"Look son this is what you do. When the girls come in this morning, they will instruct you on what you have to do and make sure you make no cock ups is that clear. It's really easy, so off you go now and tell Michael to put someone else in the cellar and that I told you to notify him."

145

Just before the pub opened that morning, two haggard-looking women, each over 40 years of age and carrying small suitcases, arrived at the back door and were admitted by Mrs Bethel, the Landlady's mother. She escorted them to the tiny store-cum-changing room at the far end of the kitchen and shouted for me to meet them and to introduce myself as their new assistant. She laughed as she announced my new status. It was apparent that Ken had primed her as to my new temporary job in the pub. I made my way to the changing room and gently knocked on the door where a voice from within instructed me to enter. That voice sounded if it had spent the previous evening smoking endless fags and gargling large glasses of brandy or neat gin. I walked in and immediately my mouth fell wide open. One of the ladies was sitting in a chair wearing tiny knickers and nothing else. Just knickers. Not even shoes.

"Alright, Son," said she as she winked at me whilst fondling her pendulous breasts and moving her milky white legs back and forth.

"Close your mouth, Son, or you might swallow a fly. Would you be a dear and get me a large gin and soda from the bar and a double whisky for Marge here as well. Now off with you before I slap your cute little bottom," both of them letting out shrieks of laughter.

"Do you want ice with the drinks?" I mumbled, although my words were barely audible.

"Naw, you're alright, luv," she chirped, and with that I fumbled for the doorknob and went to prepare the drinks. Michael was in the bar stocking the shelves and smiled.

When I returned to the changing room carrying a tray with the two glasses of alcohol balanced on my left hand, I entered without knocking. Marge, the older of the two, was sitting with one leg crossed over the other and was completely naked. She was a big girl in every sense, especially, the curly bits in the downstairs department. The tray seemed to wobble in my hands but I just about held onto it much to the amusement of the two giggling ladies.

"Have you ever seen a naked girl before, Son?" said Betty, who was still in her skimpy knickers and smoking a cigarette.

"Yea, of course, I have. Many times, in fact, if you must know," I responded lying through my teeth of course.

"Yep, lots of time," I tried to say with some confidence but I could feel my face going really red. Both women looked at each other and giggled.

"Ken instructed me to ask what I have to do for you when you are on stage and doing your act. Can you give me a clue please?" I blurted out the words as I handed over the drinks, my hands shaking.

"Well, luv, it's like this: after the music starts, when it's each of our turn to entertain the customers you lead us to the little stage in the far corner where we perform our act and when we start our routine and take our gear off, it's your job to make sure that no perv picks them up and legs it. Then, when the act is over, your escort each of us back here carrying all of our garments. And I mean all of them. Got that?"

I looked from one to the other and back again but was unable to form a response for a few seconds. They just sat staring at me. I tried desperately not to look at their naughty bits.

"I think so, miss. Yes, I'm really sure I understand," I replied nodding my head and close to breaking out in a cold sweat.

"Yes, I understand perfectly. I have to make sure that all your clothes, I mean gear, is collected after you take them off and to make absolutely certain that I bring them back to you after the show. Yep I think I have it," I replied as a tiny piece of sick rose into my mouth.

"That's a good boy. You will go far now get out of here whilst we get our faces on for the show," said Marge, sucking on an even longer cigarette than her artiste colleague and blowing me a kiss. I had to visit the toilet immediately afterwards. I wasn't very long though.

Shortly afterwards, on the recommendation from Michael, I changed into a neat white shirt and some grey trousers that Mrs B. had bought for me in Turnpike Lane, the previous Saturday. I presented myself to the artistes in the changing room for their approval as their Strippers Assistant. I watched as Big Betty, whose stage name was Divine, pulled a long black cape over her shoulders and down her back partially covering her costume for her forthcoming act. She looked sensational. I had never seen so much glitter on one person at any one time, not that I was a glitter expert. She took one long pull of her cigarette and announced in her deepest Cockney accent, "Let's go, my fine young man, lead on," and off we went through a narrow walkway and into the packed saloon bar. The audience, eager to see the Great Divine accompanied by her very nervous protector a few feet in front of the smiling artiste, clapped and whistled as I led Divine to the stage. I was shaking so much that I almost wet myself.

As Divine mounted the tiny stage, she nodded to Dave the DJ, who was at the rear working his turntable, and then pointed to a spot where I was to stand in order to collect the myriad items of her costume that she would be discarding during her performance. The music started.

"Hey, Big Spender," bellowed from the speakers at which point Divine commenced gyrating around the stage having very quickly offloaded the black cloak that she hurled in my direction and, fortunately, I was able to catch and hold on to for dear life. Then disaster happened. Divine took off her shiny bra. For a moment I was totally distracted at the sight of her wobbly breasts that appeared to have sparkly little tassels covering her nipples. As she launched the discarded bra in my general direction, she began twirling the nipple tassels clockwise at what appeared to be some considerable speed. Everything appeared to be in slow motion, apart from the twirling tassels. The bra that she had thrown in my general direction seemed to hang for ages and then dropped near the tables directly in front of me where an aged punter made a dive for the shiny, sweat-covered garment. Divine glared at me with a 'look that would kill' as I stood there transfixed whilst the perv sniffed the errant bra. The thought that she might kill me if I lost her precious bra spurred me into action. I ran towards the culprit and a tugging match commenced. He held tight and I pulled tighter and eventually the bra came my way much to the bitter disappointment of the lecherous audience member. There was a round of applause and quite a bit of laughter from some of the punters nearby. Divine was not best pleased. But she was a trooper, which is how she referred to herself, and simply continued gyrating to the music.

The music changed to *Let's Get It On* by Marvin Gaye, by which time Divine had removed the tassels and instead of throwing them to me, she dropped them on the stage behind her where she would collect them at the end of her act. Her trust in me had obviously gone.

The act finished with the total unveiling of Divine, apart from a sparkly thong that did little to cover her downstairs bits. When the music stopped and the clapping and whistling had died down, Divine beckoned me to bring over the black cape which I did and nervously draped it around her shoulders. To yet more ecstatic applause, she quickly walked through the crowd deftly avoiding potential gropes from a number of eager, slightly pissed punters. I followed behind her carrying the discarded, and by now slightly soiled pieces of her stage costume. Once in the changing room the completely naked Betty glared at me for a few seconds and then reached for her drink and took a long slug.

"Don't you do that to me ever again, you stupid boy. What are you?" I looked to the ground, hoping it would open but it didn't.

"I'm really sorry Miss. I promise it won't happen again, honest and cross my heart and hope to die." Betty looked at me, the anger in her eyes now dissipating somewhat and walked towards me. She put a hand on each side of my slightly pubic hair face, pulled me towards her and kissed me full on the lips.

"You're a good boy, but you have a lot to learn. Now off you go. And don't forget Marge needs escorting to the stage in 40 minutes. That's a good boy and don't drop her knickers or she'll skin you alive." It was just then that I decided that I was in love with a well-endowed ageing stripper called Divine. Sometime later I escorted Marge to the stage through a crowd even more fuelled with alcohol than before but the discarding of her clothing went ahead without a hitch. When we returned to the dressing room, she thanked me with a sweaty kiss on the cheek and a slap on the arse as I exited the room.

Later that evening when I had some time to myself, I asked Mrs B if I could use her phone to ring my mother. She agreed, of course. I dialled the number and I could hear the faint but unmistakable voice of Felix.

"Is that you, cub?" said he.

"Aye Daddy, how are you doing?" I replied.

"Just grand cub. Grand indeed. There's plenty of bother around here these days and you're well out of it. Are you enjoying yourself in that big city?" his hushed voice replied.

'' I am Da and really love the place but I miss home to be honest.'' I replied.

"Well, you keep out of bother over there and you'll do well. There's nothing here for the likes of young ones like you. Do you want to speak to your Mother? She's right here beside me now," as I heard him hand over the phone to Cassie Ann.

"Is that you, Son? Are they treating you well over there, those English ones?" she said hurriedly with a hint of a quiver in her voice. Cassie Ann didn't like speaking on the phone and would only do so if it was an emergency.

"Terrific, Mammy, really well aye. I love it over here and the people are great. Have a respectable job and a great place to sleep and they feed me into the bargain." I gushed hoping that she wouldn't detect the emotion in my voice.

"That's good, cub. I am happy for you Son and pray every night that God looks down on you. I must be going now because these things are wild expensive (meaning the cost of telephone call) and I don't want to get you into any bother. Write me a wee letter when you have the time. God Bless now and don't forget to go to Mass every Sunday and say your prayers before you go to bed. And Son, you heed my words and don't be going anywhere near those dirty auld English girls. You might catch something bad." And with that final piece of motherly advice, the phone went dead. It was a Sunday evening in London. I had missed Mass yet again and during the afternoon, I was escorting strippers to a stage in a seedy pub in Palmers Green and watching them as they took their clothes off and displaying parts of the female anatomy that I had never seen up close before. If Cassie Ann had known the truth of that day, I would have been excommunicated from the Catholic Church and very probably disowned forever.

For an acne-ridden young man, from a strict Irish Catholic background, it was an experience that I could never have envisaged even in my wildest or horniest of dreams. For the next two years, every Wednesday evening and Sunday morning, there I was, the Strippers Assistant in the Cock Tavern, an occupation that Cassie Ann would never find out about. Felix did not have any idea either as to my unlikely occupation, although I think he might just have understood and been forgiving. And for some peculiar reason, my acne cleared up shortly after that first meeting with the two ageing performers and my introduction to the world of strippers.

Now working in the Cock Tavern, both as a barman and my twice-weekly role as the Stripper's Assistant, was to see life away from the brutality and thuggery of that world I had left behind in the small provincial town where I was born and desperately tried to grow up. At weekends, if I had a few days off, some English lads who had befriended me whilst drinking in the bar, would take me to the West End to chase after girls or to White Hart Lane to watch Tottenham Hotspur. My life had changed so much for the better and was now worth living. And as for girls, they were everywhere and easily approached and they didn't even ask whether I was a Protestant or a Catholic. Mrs B., however, was very protective when it came to allowing girls into the living quarters in the pub and always firmly demanded that any physical contact with the opposite sex be conducted elsewhere. There was no resentment in my behalf as I understood just how much she had done for me and I was never going to break her trust in me and upset her.

However, there was one unfortunate incident that took place in the ladies changing rooms. Not long into my role as the assistant to the artistes, I was asked to take some drinks to one of the regulars, Big Betty whom I was fond of as she used to tip me, and a new girl called Josie whose stage name was Trixibelle.

As I enter the changing room, I could hear Big Betty using the toilet at the rear of the room. The new girl Josie who was seated near the dressing table slowly turned around and allowed her short red dressing gown to come undone, showing lots of cleavage and very scant underwear.

"Thank you, my young man. You seem such a sweet boy. Betty has been telling me all about you. Come over here and sit right down beside me" as she patted the seat next to her.

''I don't bite darling. Unless you really insist sweetie," she started laughing whilst continuously stroking her hair with her right hand.

"Here's your drink, Ms Trixibelle," said I whilst trying to keep a steady hold of the drinks tray.

"You can call me Josie, dear boy, and none of that Miss nonsense. In fact, you can call me anything you desire, if you wish. Now don't be nervous with me and let's have that drink before you spill it," gushed Josie, who by now was looking like the most beautiful woman that I had ever seen even if she was over 40 and had a few wrinkles around her neck. All of a sudden, she arose from her seat and quickly approached me. There was just the drinks tray between the two of us. I handed over the glass of alcohol with a trembling hand and put the tray on the chair beside me.

"Oops, the ice is melting," she murmured whilst sipping the drink. "You must be very hot. Do you have a girlfriend, you sweet young man?"

"No. Well not really, Miss Josie. I have too many things going on with my job and all."

"But you must relax sometimes, you hunk of a man. And you are so handsome and so strong. Tell me, do you like what you see?" As she moved even closer to me, the sweat almost running down the inside of my legs. Or at least I think it was sweat.

"Oh, I do, Miss. Very much indeed, Miss. You are beautiful." I replied with a flushed face and my hands shaking. God knows where that came from.

"Right then, young man. I need a bit of help with my bra strap. It keeps catching me under the breast. Join me in the toilet over there just in case some nosey parker wanders in and thinks we are up to no good. If you know what I mean. They might think something naughty is going on and, of course, it isn't. Is it? You are such a young gentleman, aren't you? Now give me your hand, you sweet young thing."

I had no option but to take her hand and follow her into the alternative toilet as the luscious Miss Josie Trixibelle totally bewitched me.

Just then the door of the lavatory opened and Betty entered the changing room. She looked at me and then towards Josie and winked extravagantly at her.

"He is a lovely boy though. But we'll have to keep an eye on him, eh Josie?" said Betty lighting another cigarette and rearranging her pants before walking into the bar for a drink with some of the punters and possibly to pick up some extra cash from one of them who fancied his chances after the pub was closed for the night.

"A girl got to make the most of it whilst she's got it," was her nightly comment after she had finished her act and returned to the dressing room.

With only the two of us in the changing room, Josie decided that I needed a kiss and put down the cigarette that she had just lit.

"You can have me if you are really quick. Would you like that?" said Josie, just inches from my sweaty face whilst running her right hand up and down my leg.

"Oh, Miss Josie, you are just, you know, divine! I think I am falling in love with you," I mumbled into her ear, the smell of her perfume almost making me sneeze.

"Make love to me here and now. I can't wait. Do it. Do it to me," her voice rising in anticipation.

I held her close and as she touched me down below, I felt something wet happening in my pants.

"I love you…" I squealed with ecstasy although still wearing my trousers.

Josie pulled away rapidly and glared at me.

"You stupid little boy. What have you done? Get out of here this instant, you silly bloody virgin."

After I escorted her to the stage and performed my duties by catching her sweaty knickers and bra and followed her to the changing room not a word was said. I never saw Josie again after that terrible evening. Somehow, Mrs B found out about the incident resulting in Josie never returning to the Cock Tavern. Mrs B never mentioned anything to me but I knew to never again fall for the allure and charms of a stripper, beautiful or not.

The Square Mile

Mrs Bethell never had any children. She treated me as if I was one of her own and without any discussion between us decided that I was to be her unofficial adopted son. I may have been gangly and very spotty but Ann Bethell had made up her mind that I was to be the precious son that she could never have. I was pampered and given free rein on my comings and goings but she also ensured that any female company that I might attract was fully vetted at the earliest. Living in a strip pub in North London had its attractions, and indeed many distractions, but Mrs Bethell made it absolutely clear that I shouldn't stray too far from home. It was her avowed ambition to make sure that I was to become someone that she would help and to be proud of.

After a few months of working in the Cock, Mrs B arranged an interview for me with one of the regulars, a very well-spoken, distinguished old gentleman who just happened to be the General Manager of a fund management company in the City of London, the financial district known as the Square Mile in the heart of the City. After a long chat one evening, he suggested that I visit him in his office for an interview about a role as an office junior in the unit trust department of his company. The following Monday morning at 8 am, I caught the number 224 bus from Palmers Green Garage direct to Moorgate and entered into a world about which I knew absolutely nothing. The interview went well and I was introduced to a number of members of staff and was told to appear the following Monday at 9 am prompt. I found my way back to the Cock and rushed into to see Mrs B and told her the good news. She hugged me. I had a job, a real job. In the City of London of all places.

After my induction on that first morning of my new role which entailed lots of menial tasks it wasn't long before I was sat with the team whose job was to calculate the daily prices for each of the funds managed by the firm. For ages I did not have a clue as to the strange language that was constantly in use and was even required to learn how to read the Financial Times which was a challenge for someone whose daily reading material about stretched to the Daily Mirror. Eventually this strange new world began to draw me in. After about a year I was given a position on their dealing desk, collating various statistics on market movements and price changes and finally I began to have a grasp of how everything worked in that strange but fascinating industry. Every working day was a suit day. Even though I was still a junior I was well paid and still living and working part time in the Cock. Mrs B refused to accept any rent and spent far too much money on buying me new clothes and expensive shoes.

"If you are going to work with those posh people, you are going to have to look the part, Son," she would say and then take me to the expensive men's shop in Palmers Green the following Saturday morning to buy me a new suit. She always chose the suit and would insist on me strutting up and down the shop floor in it to make sure I looked good. There was never any argument from me about her selection as she was just the classiest of women. Mrs B had become my English mother but Cassie Ann would always be my real life, noisy and very funny Mammy in Ireland.

I remained with that unit trust company for several years before being enticed to a posh merchant bank based in Old Broad Street close to the London Stock Exchange in Throgmorton Avenue. The bank was known as Samuel Montagu. It was founded in the 1850s as a brokerage firm for bullion dealing. Samuel Montagu's chairman at them time was a very rotund individual who owned a terrier named Montagu, which would travel with him in the back seat of his chauffeur-driven Mercedes. It was to be a fascinating next few years in an institution staffed by individuals where double-barrelled names were the norm.

By this time, Mrs B and her randy husband Ken had sold the Cock Tavern and moved to a small country pub in Kent. I would visit with them occasionally but life had moved on and so did I. The very last time I had visited Mrs B she walked me to the railway station and as we were awaiting the train's arrival, she held my left hand really tight, turned to me and winked.

"Look after yourself, my fine big man, and don't forget what I taught you. Don't let the bastards ever get you down." I hugged her close for a few minutes and then left her standing at the door. She was crying. And so was I. That was the last time that I ever saw Mrs B.

I was the only member of staff at that prestigious merchant bank located in the City of London that had a distinct accent. The vast majority of the employees had accents that could best be described as posh with all of them emanating from London or the Home Counties, as opposed to the Six Counties. The City of London is the financial centre of the UK and covers just over one square mile. It stretches from Temple to the Tower of London on the River Thames and from west to east that includes Chancery Lane and Liverpool Street. The Square Mile is home to the London the Stock Exchange, the Bank of England, Mansion House where the Lord Mayor resides, and a host of financial institutions including banks and stockbrokers, all out to make a profit from gullible investors and greedy speculators.

A merchant bank is historically a bank dealing in commercial loans and investments however, the bulk of its profits were generated through gold bullion dealing where huge volumes of the precious metal were kept secure in vaults beneath the building. For a brief period, I was required to work in the bullion department where shipments were despatched and delivered on a daily basis. Every evening there would be a requirement for an audit of the gold bars, the silver and gold coins including Krugerrands and any mistakes not tolerated. After a few months it became quite boring and tiresome but someone had to account for the weighty lumps of metal and I was just one of many tasked with the job. Sadly, the bars were so heavy that it was nigh impossible to sneak one down your pants and out the door at the end of the day's counting.

In modern British usage a merchant bank is now the same as an investment bank. Apart from bullion dealing its main activities were promoting companies that wished to list on the Stock Market or to assist with acquisitions and mergers. The bank's offices in Old Broad Street were staffed with ex-public-school types, mainly men, most of whom had surnames that could have been lifted directly from some obscure Bertie Wooster novels. A few 'Richards' but certainly lots of 'Dicks'. There was also the occasional titled individual who was merely biding his time until his father popped his clogs and he could then take over the family estate and his seat in the House of Lords. Bit different from the town where I grew up and a world of unemployment and never-ending bitterness between two religious factions. In the City the only deity was money and many worshipped at its altar. My accent always attracted snide comments from my work colleagues. I would try to dismiss them but there was always the impression given that being Irish meant we were supposed to be entertaining and always able to 'take a joke' at our own expense. Nonetheless, working in such an environment where the salary was good and the staff benefits excellent, was both exciting and stimulating and very different from picking up some old stripper's discarded knickers.

One late morning I entered the lift on the ground floor of the bank at the same time as a Board Director and his wife. They had followed me into the lift where the Director proceeded to press the button that would take them both up to the executive dining rooms at the top of the building. I recognised both him and his wife whose pictures were often seen in the national press. He was the Honourable

Angus Ogilvy, married to Princess Alexandra, first cousin to the Queen, and a man who was later involved in a notorious scandal involving the breaking of trade sanctions imposed by the UK against Rhodesia, now Zimbabwe. It was known as the Lonhro Affair and resulted in Angus, Gus to his friends but not to minions like me, having to resign most of his City directorships apart from a few select ones such as those at Sotheby's and GEC. A few years after the scandal, the Queen made him a Knight Commander of the Royal Victorian Order and subsequently, he was appointed a Privy Councillor. At least it gave him more time to spend with his Princess wife, beside whom I was now standing in a lift in Old Broad Street. Without asking, I leant across him to press the button for my floor, one that was far below the heady heights of the executive dining room. He was smoking a cigarette and smiled at me as I cautiously stood back after pressing the button. I looked directly at him and for whatever stupid reason forgot his name and simply said, "It's yourself then."

He turned very slightly in my direction, took a pull of his cigarette, and to the great amusement of his overdressed Princess, he replied, "Indeed it is, dear boy. Indeed, it is." All was silent until the door to my floor opened and I exited. The Princess smiled at me as I turned back to say thanks and my face, as per bloody usual, went bright scarlet red. Angus Ogilvy may have come from landed gentry and he appeared to be a gracious man with great personal charm but to me he looked like a man who never had to dig spuds for his dinner.

Years later I was very fortunate to be hired by a large fund management company whose offices were based near St Paul's Cathedral where the opportunities to entertain clients and live life to the full were endless. Most senior members of staff were provided with a company credit card and access to expense accounts that were constantly in use in the many City wine bars and flash restaurants all in pursuit of new clients and the revenue that would be generated for their firms. In order to poach clients, entertainment would take the form of not just wining and dining in upmarket restaurants but also in private boxes at prestige racecourses such as Sandown and Ascot or a few days of golf in St Andrews in Scotland. As long as the business kept rolling in the doors of our employers the approval of our expense claims was never an issue. The City of London revolved around entertaining and being entertained at the expense of your firm or someone else's.

On one memorable occasion we were on the receiving end of the largesse of a major bank, the soon-to-be disgraced Royal Bank of Scotland ('RBS'). Their role was to ensure that the fund management assets for which investors had paid far too much were protected by the bank. Their client-facing representatives had access to serious company credit cards with which to woo their existing and potential new clients and to ensure that everyone had a really enjoyable time. And we certainly did. Repeatedly, all under the pretext of 'client entertainment', we enjoyed their hospitality. Every opportunity to entertain clients was taken. Whether it was a private room in an up-market wine bar in the City of London to celebrate Burns Night or an afternoon's drinking of the finest wines whilst watching the racing from Cheltenham in a cordoned-off section of a posh restaurant, the RBS team would wave their gold cards with great abandon.

Such was the generosity of our hosts for one event, a number of us were invited to a swanky wine bar called Balls Brothers that was located on a street just off Mayfair. This was in Brook Street, the London version. Sitting at a table overflowing with expensive wines and bottles of port and watching the non-stop consumption of liquor and food I briefly thought back to those days in that other Brook Street where Hannah Shannon fed her squealing pigs and collected leftovers in her wheelbarrow. 'Have you any brock this day' she used to shout in between taking a drag of a cigarette butt that she held at the side of her mouth. 'My pigs need feeding' she would holler as she walked down Brook Street pushing her box on old pram wheels. I went home that evening and thought about how ridiculous we were sitting in a fancy wine bar and not a care in the world. A world so ill-divided.

It was whilst working at Samuel Montagu that I received the phone call from a near neighbour on the Derry Road who insisted that I make my way home as soon as possible. Cassie Ann was not well and it was best for me to return home without delay. She was a tough woman and surely there was nothing to be concerned about. Cassie Ann was too young to die and had so much to live for. Sadly, I was to be proved wrong.

Funerals

Funerals are at their best when celebrated by a priest who does a 'good' Mass. Those attending will still be talking about what a lovely ceremony it was many months later and "Doesn't he do a lovely funeral and doesn't that priest have a lovely voice. That wee priest is just an angel. Jesus, I hope he is still around when it's my turn."

The priest in his black or purple vestments would recite prayers from the Missal as he leads the cortege slowly into the church with the coffin carried on the shoulders of six men. The tradition is that the deceased is borne headfirst through the door as it is considered bad luck the other way around so great care is taken to ensure that it is carried the correct way. From the hearse parked directly outside the entrance to the church the coffin is taken up to the altar rails whilst the congregation stands in silence. Unlike some cultures the lid of the coffin remains closed in the church, the mourners and family having spent the previous two nights waking the deceased 'on show' in the home house. Had the person been a member of some local organisation such as the Irish National Foresters or, on rare occasions, Sinn Fein, occasionally a flag would be draped over the coffin.

The Requiem Mass is usually an hour-long ceremony but if the priest likes the sound of his own voice or, if the eulogy is an endless history of the deceased and his charitable deeds and care for the poor, especially if he or she was a respected dignitary of the town, then a monotonous cleric could send the congregation into a peaceful slumber. Particularly for the close relatives who would have had very little sleep during the preceding two nights of the Wake. No matter how bad a scoundrel the deceased may have been there is never a bad word said about the occupant of the casket irrespective of any skulduggery and debauchery during their lifetime. It always behoves the celebrant of the Requiem Mass to provide an endorsement of the recently deceased with such speeches as 'this good and decent Catholic has served his dues and should be admitted through the gates of the Heaven without delay'. Sadly, not all would be successful in gaining admission into the abode of saints.

The origin of the Wake probably dates back to the ancient Jewish custom of leaving the sepulchre, or burial chamber, of a recently departed relative, unsealed for three days before finally closing it up, during which time family members would visit frequently in the hope of seeing signs of a return to life. From time to time, the expression 'I have never seen him/her look so well' would be heard by friends whilst viewing the deceased albeit there was never a return to the land of the living. Of course, a good undertaker was worth his weight in gold especially if he could enhance the look of the deceased for those few days and nights of public viewing.

In rural Ireland, according to tradition, a Wake is seen as the glorious send-off of a departed loved one and an opportunity for friends and neighbours to pay their respects to the family of the recently deceased. Wakes have been a prominent feature of Irish funeral traditions for many centuries but is seen less often in modern Ireland and is now almost unknown in the cities. However, in many country areas such as in rural Tyrone, Donegal and Fermanagh, the practice of watching over the recently deceased from the time of death to burial is still followed and is an important part of the grieving process. It is the reason why many Irish funerals, outside of the cities, are still preceded by a Wake, lasting a minimum of two nights with the burial of the deceased on the third day usually after 10 or 11 am Mass. Signs are erected by the undertaker and placed at crossroads and at intersections pointing to the Wake House so that visitors from distant parts of the county are directed to the right location and do not have to bother neighbours by asking directions.

Drinks, arguments, greed and family feuds play a major part in the waking process, especially where money and land are involved. As the night rolls on and if the opportunity arises, music and mayhem would invariably break out during the early hours when spirits were sagging and even more spirits consumed. In the past cigarettes were made available on saucers and left in strategic places where those who enjoyed a smoke could help themselves without having to bother anyone.

Traditionally, the Wake takes place in the family home of the deceased with the body 'presented' in an ornate casket and is considered a formal social celebration of the person's life. Visitors come and go at all hours where there is endless handshaking and lots of 'sorry for your trouble' and 'God will be good to him/her.' The deceased is dressed in his or her finest suit or dress and is laid out in the coffin in the best room of the house—the one reserved for visitors, especially the priests and nuns who would visit for tea on rare occasions and the occasional handout if it was offered. The period of mourning would last for two full days and nights with friends, neighbours and relatives visiting the family to pay their last respects and to hear and share the local gossip. If the death was of natural causes, the coffin would invariably be left open and the body of the deceased covered with Mass cards and rosary beads and small bottles of holy water from Knock Shrine.

During this waking process endless cups of tea would be drunk, sandwiches with the edges curling eaten and a never-ending supply of cigarettes inhaled.

Often the most memorable part of the Wake—and the most comforting for the family—would be the anecdotes and stories.

"Did I ever tell you about the time that we fell in the ditch and him steaming drunk and his Mammy chased us across the fields when we climbed out," they would begin and very probably not shut up for the next three hours depending upon how much drink had been taken.

Old friends and relatives would exaggerate tales about the life of the deceased, interspersed with laughter and tears. His or her love of slow horses or Bingo, or his support for some English football team that he has never seen in the flesh. After a few drinks, the topic would invariably turn to the deceased's choice of spouse, whether he was 'good to her' or 'she was above her station'. Or if there was no spouse there would be stories of lost love or tales of heartbreak. Stories would overlap and others would flow from them until one of the mourners would take it upon himself that it was time for a song or two— usually a maudlin ballad sung out of tune due to the enormous consumption of strong drink.

Every Wake has them. The funeral version of the bridesmaid or groomsman. The invaluable organiser and referee of any rows or fights that might break out. Behind the scenes, they help coordinate the food, clean the cups, talk to the priest, top up the drinks, pick up the rubbish and diplomatically, eject any drunks or unwelcome guests from the house. They do it all quietly and without fuss. They will not let you know which cake they baked or sandwiches they prepared, they will always have tissues for the tearful and the nose blowers and they are there when a grieving relative has had enough of the evening and wants to lie down somewhere quiet. They go unnoticed but are indispensable at a packed Wake house. When the crowds are gone and the house needs cleaning, it is she, invariably always a woman, who arranges it all, quietly and without fuss. Our organiser for Cassie Ann's Wake was the sister-in-law, Sally, a nurse by profession and wife of the older brother. Calm and efficient, she quietly and efficiently arranged the food, the endless tea, the escorting to the visitors to the house and barring the occasional drunk looking for more alcohol after the pubs were closed.

Some Wakes can be uproarious especially if the deceased was a local character who enjoyed life. One infamous Wake was that of Jimmy Fee, a rotund jolly little man with very few teeth, whose occupation was that of a horse dealer and a breeder of donkeys. He passed away at the ripe old age of 79 and, as was the local tradition, his remains were laid out in the coffin in the front room of his own little house, not far from Brook Street, for visitors to pay their last respects. His reputation for dealing in animals was known far and wide and thus his demise attracted many mourners especially from the farming and horse breeding communities. It was the liveliest of Wakes with endless drinking, including an illegal brew made from grain or potatoes called Poitin, also known as Poteen. It is a lethal drink at the best of times and usually drunk accompanied by endless bottles of Guinness.

The mourners were having such a grand time drinking, storytelling and singing that they decided to prolong the Wake. In the early hours of the morning of the funeral, the coffin was removed from the house by his close friends in life, placed on the back of a lorry and driven to a secret location in the remote countryside. The Wake continued into the following day with the same great gusto and consumption of alcohol. The Parish Priest, a man who frowned upon such behaviour was a stickler for punctuality and acting on a tip-off from a concerned relative, turned up at the hideaway and read his version of the Riot Act to the assembled, and by now very drunk, mourners.

The Requiem Mass was performed that morning at 10 0'clock and the internment of the deceased Jimmy Fee, breeder of slow horses and renowned donkey dealer, took place immediately afterwards in Drumragh Cemetery under the ever-watchful eyes of the furious Parish Priest. To their credit Jimmy's mourners continued with their drinking and carousing for several days after the burial of the immortal friend.

Wakes in rural Ireland were not to be missed. And no invite or RSVP required.

Her final farewell

During those days of austerity and sectarianism, it was not unusual for men and women to die relatively young and the passing of Cassie Ann, whilst devastating for the family, it was not a shock. The doctor said an enlarged heart was the cause of death which seemed appropriate. She had an enormously generous heart, in fact, and one that enveloped everyone she ever encountered. Her Wake was an occasion of great celebration rather than the normal mourning and grieving. Many country people came from far and wide to pay their last respects during the Wake and to scc for one last time a woman who embodied all that was good and decent in a person.

Cassie Ann passed away at the age of 64. She had died shortly before I arrived home and I had missed the opportunity to finally say goodbye to her and to thank her for giving me a chance in life. She was still in the morgue, so I insisted upon driving there to see her and to pay my respects in private. Cassie Ann's body was wrapped in a white sheet and placed in a tin receptacle to await the undertaker who would look after her remains and arrange her in the coffin. I stood beside that tin box and looked at her sallow features and the shrivelled lips and tried desperately not to scream in front of the young nurse who had accompanied me to the morgue. Rigor mortis had not commenced and her hands were not yet cold, so I held her right hand, the one that I shook that day I left her at the front door to travel to London and my bright new future in that big bad world. Standing in a morgue looking down at the lifeless body of your mother and simultaneously feeling lost and confused, is a rite of passage for so many sons and daughters when their parents die but it is not one that we look forward to or ever envisage. I gently brushed back her greying curly hair so that I could kiss her on the forehead and turned to the nurse for whom I shall be forever grateful for her dignity and compassion.

On the first night of the Wake, there was a never-ending parade of friends and neighbours coming through the front door all to pay their final respects and have a cup of tea and a sandwich or something stronger. After the mandatory handshakes, the mourner would approach the coffin and make the Sign of the Cross followed by a short prayer over the body of the deceased. Death is an inexorable part of every community and culture yet, despite how harsh death is, nonetheless such events can surprisingly unite people and bring them closer to their friends and relatives. A distant cousin or long-lost uncle who may not have crossed the threshold in years will suddenly reappear to mourn with the rest of the family. Because Cassie Ann had an aunt in the Loreto Convent in the town, small groups of nuns appeared at various times of the evening and after saying prayers over Cassie Ann and sympathising with the family, they would sit on chairs placed around the walls of the Wake room and chat about her life and her departed aunt, Sister Martha. On such occasions, alcohol would not be made available and those who may have been imbibing remained in the kitchen or in the backyard drinking and smoking and annoying the two mongrel dogs.

During the second evening of the Wake, one of the Catholic curates put in his mandatory appearance. Yet more handshakes with the relatives and neighbours and then yet another recital of the Rosary. This lengthy series of prayers is said on multiple occasions during the two evenings of the Wake but not always to an appreciative audience especially those who may have had a drink or two. There are only so many times that one can recite 'Holy Mary, Mother of God, pray for us now and at the hour of our death' before the words become meaningless and the mourners consumed with exhaustion.

Mirrors in the front room where Cassie was reposing, were covered with a white sheet or turned inwards to the wall and the hands on the clock in the room were stopped as a sign of respect and to avoid bad luck. If possible, the clock is stopped at the estimated time of death. The curtains were closed and holy candles lit at various points around the room. And then there was food. Lots of food. Even though we were not in the slightest bit hungry. Grief has a wonderful way of stemming the hunger pains. The neighbours rallied around and delivered sandwiches, always cut into triangles, a multiple array of iced buns and goodness knows how many burnt mini sausage rolls. And endless cups of teas were poured with which to wash down the ham and cheese sandwiches.

Jimmy Friel, who owned the local pub, sent across several cases of Guinness and a couple of bottles of Bushmills Whisky with which to sustain the mourners during the long night hours and to lubricate their throats for the singing and storytelling. And indeed, in the wee small hours of the night, when sleep was required, many songs were sung and stories told all in memory of the big-hearted woman from Donegal who touched the lives of so many and gave what little she possessed to those in greater need than herself and her family.

On that last night, I sat beside her inexpensive softwood coffin and watched over her still body. Her well-used Rosary Beads were entwined through her cold nail-bitten fingers, her shrouded body surrounded by Mass Cards and small bottles of unopened Lourdes Holy Water randomly scattered throughout the coffin. She still wore her wedding band and had her false teeth inserted in her mouth which gave her the appearance of grinning in her sleep. The National Health prescription glasses had been dispensed with which made her face seem quite serene. The lifelong burden of worries and fears had now been removed from the heart and soul of her short, tormented life. Finally, Cassie Ann was at peace.

Doherty the Undertaker was the man to whom all locals turned when a death occurred in the family. Catholic funerals are distinctive in that they follow certain protocols that must be rigidly adhered to and Doherty knew them intimately. On the morning of the funeral, the hearse drew up outside the house an hour before Mass began. The Wake was now over and the time for Cassie Ann's last journey to the Sacred Heart Church, her daily place of worship, was imminent. Her coffin rested upon on a trestle table in the front room, the sitting room, and surrounded by close family and friends. The Undertaker recited the Rosary with the small gathering answering the prayers until its conclusion and finally, the coffin lid put in place and sealed ready to be carried out of the house and inserted into the rear of the long black hearse. Her mongrel dog, the farting testicle licker, suddenly started yelping from the back yard as if to say its farewell in the only way a dog can which is to bark and howl. It received a kick in the arse and was hurriedly removed into the back yard.

We marched in pairs behind the hearse as it slowly made its way over the brow of the hill and up through Castle Street and eventually, it came to a stop in front of the Church where the Celebrant was waiting with prayer book in his hands and a young altar boy gently swinging an incense holder, called a thurible, back and forth that emitted a mist over the coffin. A large crowd had gathered making the Sign of the Cross as they stood in silence watching the coffin being carried up the aisle by members of the family, myself included, and gently placed on a stand immediately in front of the main altar. And now, for this one time only, she had pride of place at the front of the altar in her beloved Sacred Heart Church, a place where she so rightfully belonged. And no black mongrel dog licking its privates and farting at her feet!

As Cassie Ann was not born in the local parish, she was interred in a new cemetery aptly named Greenhills, about a mile outside the town. She now rests there with Felix at her side and within sight of her adopted home. At long last she was at peace.

Death in a Small Town

On the afternoon of Saturday 15th August 1998 at 3.10 pm, a car filled with explosives was detonated in the centre of a small country town killing 29 people including two unborn children as well as injuring 370 people. It remains the largest loss of life of any single incident in the history of the Northern Ireland Troubles. Numerous telephone warnings had been sent by the bombers some 40 minutes prior to the explosion, but the directions were inaccurate and, inadvertently, the RUC had moved people towards the Vauxhall Cavalier containing the mass of explosives parked at the bottom end of the town.

Glass, masonry and metal tore through the crowd on the street as a fireball swept out from the epicentre of the bomb. Twenty-one people were killed instantly—some of their bodies were never found intact, such was the force of the blast. A water main under the road ruptured resulting in gallons of water gushing out on to the road. Some of the dead and badly injured were washed down the hill such was the volume of water from the fractured main.

On that fateful day, the Feast of the Assumption a day that is celebrated by Catholics worldwide, the car was driven into Omagh but as the town was busy the driver was unable to find a parking spot near the intended target, the Court House. He then drove to the bottom of Market Street, the main thoroughfare, and parked in front of S D Kells, a clothes shop, and together with his accomplice primed the bomb and then casually walked to a waiting car driven by another accomplice.

Prior to the explosion numerous calls were made to a television station and the Samaritans warning of the impending explosion but providing the wrong location. This resulted in the police evacuating everyone from the vicinity of the Court House and instead of sending them to safety people were ushered towards the vehicle carrying the explosives. Forty minutes after the initial telephone warning the bomb was detonated. Libby, our near neighbour and died instantly. Libby was 57 years of age and married to her soulmate Laurence who passed away several years later of a broken heart. Amongst the dead were 2 Spanish tourists aged 12 and 23 who had been on a daytrip to the town. Of the 29 people who perished that fateful day 11 were of the Protestant faith and 18 were Roman Catholics. The morning after the bombing, a man was killed when his car collided with an ambulance ferrying bomb victims to hospitals in Belfast.

Libby Rush was standing outside her coffee shop directly opposite the car containing the explosives. She was watching the commotion as the police tried to move as many people as possible away from what they assumed was the suspect vehicle that was supposedly located at the top of the town in front of the Court House. It was not their fault that the information provided by the bombers only 40 minutes beforehand was incorrect but the consequences of their action was catastrophic for so many people including Libby. The bombers had stolen the car in County Monaghan several days previously, changed the number plates to those bearing a Northern Ireland registration and loaded the vehicle with 500 pounds of fertiliser-based explosives.

The carnage created by the bomb caused outrage both nationally and internationally and had the effect of spurring on the peace process. A splinter group of the IRA, the Real IRA, claimed its target was commercial and not civilian and blamed the loss of life on the failure of the RUC to respond to 'clear' warnings. Subsequently, the Real IRA called a ceasefire to their activities. The carnage created by the bomb was to become known as the largest loss of life in a single incident during the Troubles in that Six Counties of Ireland.

Numerous arrests were made on both sides of the border with various court cases brought against those suspected of being involved in the bombing but, although the perpetrators of the outrage were found liable for the attack by a High Court judge in a civil action, there were no criminal charges proven against them. In 2001 a report by the Police Ombudsman found that the RUC Special Branch failed to act on prior warnings and heavily criticised the RUC's investigation of the bombing.

British, Irish and US intelligence agencies allegedly had information which could have prevented the bombing, most of which came from so-called double agents inside the Real IRA but this information was not given to the RUC. In 2008, the BBC reported that British intelligence agency GCHQ was monitoring conversations between the bombers as the bomb was being driven into the town. In hindsight it was obvious that the authorities knew that a bomb was destined for the area but, for whatever reason they chose, to let the bombers proceed and create havoc and misery for so many innocent people.

Not only were Catholics and Protestants murdered that fateful day but a number of Spanish tourists and several visitors from the Irish Republic died along with the beating heart of that small provincial town in North-West Ireland that was so beloved by Cassie Ann.

The name of that place was Omagh.

A view of the damage caused in Bridge Street by the car bomb.

Irish Diaspora

For centuries young men and women have been packing their bags and leaving Ireland to settle in all corners of the world. There were, and still are, many reasons for leaving. The Great Famine of the 1840s resulted in mass emigration from Ireland with approximately 2 million setting off in what were called 'coffin ships' and eventually settling in Canada and the United States. It has been estimated that over 40 million Americans now claim to have Irish heritage including many Presidential candidates irrespective of how remote the connection. Even Barack Obama laid claims of having ancestors in County Offaly, one of whom was his 7th great grandfather, Joseph Kearney.

Up until the 1950s whenever a young member of a rural family was departing for America or Canada their relations would gather in the farmhouse for what was known as the American Wake. It was assumed that the emigrant would never return to his or her homeland and hence the living wake or farewell supper. Drinking, carousing and singing mixed with many tears would continue until the early hours of the day of departure. Mothers cried for the sons and daughters whom they were well aware that they would never set eyes upon them again and hence the need for the living wake.

In later years unemployment, especially in rural areas and small provincial towns, created a roaring business for the ferries heading to Liverpool and Heysham and planes flying to London, Canada, New York, and Boston. In London, the Irish congregated in a number of areas such as Kilburn, Hammersmith, Holloway and Camden Town where there were Irish-run pubs and dancehalls such as the Gresham and the Galtymore. Emigrants would flock to these venues where they would meet and enjoy the company of their countrymen and women, if only for a few hours. And, occasionally, to marry and settle in their adopted country.

Northern Ireland, also known as the Six Counties depending upon your political or religious persuasion, has witnessed a mass exodus of young people, especially Catholics, since the creation of the state in 1921. Bigotry and discrimination have resulted in disproportionate unemployment for the minority Catholics and hence the only option was to hop on a bus to the port at Belfast or Dublin and a ferry to England and then on to Manchester, Birmingham or London in search of work and a life. The so-called Troubles from the 1970s onwards, when so much violence was perpetrated upon each community, has seen so many young people leave in search of a world without murder and mayhem and one where they could build a life for themselves. Few returned. Thankfully, the violence is nearing its end but bigotry still exists, albeit less obvious these days, and youngsters still feel the need to leave the land of their birth and their families.

Many immigrants to the big cities of England and elsewhere have been fortunate to succeed in their chosen fields or professions. Others have scraped by working on building sites, in pubs or digging underground tunnels in London, New York, Sydney and elsewhere. There have been many occasions when we have missed our mothers, the backbone of so many poor families in Ireland. Where once it was a case of the occasional letter between parent and offspring, now it is a call on the iPhone or a chat on Zoom and the miles really do not exist anymore. We never forget where we come from and, more importantly, our mothers.

The Irish Mammy is a magnificent and much-treasured institution. To most mothers their sons will always be 9 years of age, butter will never melt in their mouths and no girl will ever be good enough for them. Irish Mammies might be stereotyped but you would be hard pressed to find a more enduring symbol of Ireland.

Glossary of Terms

Ach: A regional word that's usually placed at the start of a sentence: 'Ach would you look at that one.''

Arse: Bottom, bum. "He could do with a good kick up the arse."

Aye: Yes. "Aye, I'll have a pint if you're buying."

Banter: Craic, fun chatter. "Let's go for a pint and have a bit of a banter."

Bate: To beat: ''I'll bate the shite out of you.''

Big Lad: A robust young gentleman. "Alright big lad?"

Boggin: meaning 'dirty' as in "that wee cub is boggin."

Bout Ye!: Greeting as in ''How are you.''

Boys a dear: Expression meaning ''That's hard to believe.''

Brew: Unemployment bureau. ''I see that lump is still on the brew. Never did a day's work in his life.''

Buck eejit: A halfwit or fool. 'God but he is one buck eejit that son of yours.''

C' mere: A command. "Come here you wee brat."

Catch yourself on!: An expression, translated as "Get a hold of yourself!", "Wise up!"

Ceili: Refers to traditional Irish dancing or to pop into a neighbour's house for a visit ''just popping in for a wee ceili.''

Craic: Fun, to have a good time. "She's good craic that one."

Cub: Young boy: ''That's a good cub you have there, Missus''

Cutty: Young girl: ''That cutty of yours is one bad article.''

Da: Meaning father: "I saw your Da in the pub last night. He was full."

Dander: Walk. "Let's go for a wee dander."

Dead-On: Meaning good, decent or alright. "I like him, he's dead-on."

Does my head in: Meaning annoying: ''Jesus he does my head in that brother of yours.''

Eejit : An idiot: "You are a right eejit."

Effing and blinding: Cursing. ''A few drinks and all you hear from that Missus of yours is effing this and blinding that.''

Fegs: Cigarettes. "Can I have twenty fegs and a packet of matches Mrs?''

Fiddle: A violin. "Get that fiddle out and play us a tune or two."

Fire: To throw. "I was out firing stones at the polis last night."

Full: Drunk: ''Jesus you're as full as a sheugh.''

Grand: Good. "That's grand, I'll see you at half-eleven down the pub then."

Gulpin: Ignorant or greedy. "Jesus he is one gulpin that man of yours.''

Hefted: Lifted or heaved. ''He hefted her into the back of the tractor.''

Hi boy: Greeting: 'Hi boy how's it going?'

Houl: Meaning to hold: "Your man can't houl his beer'' or "Houl my jacket while I bate the bastard.''

Hoak: Rummage: "That wee man hoaks through the bins."

Hole: Bottom or Bum: "Get your lazy hole out of that bed and go to work you wee shite."

How's about ye: A form of greeting: "How's about you Mister. Do you have any spare change?"

Hoor: A woman/man of ill repute: ''By God he is one hoor of a man.''

I tell a lie: Expression, meaning you've made an error: "I tell a lie, I do remember who you father was."

I'll do you!: Expression, meaning you're in big trouble: "I'll do you big lad, just you watch.''

Is it yerself?: Regional question: "Hello how are you?"

Is your head cut?: Expression, meaning are you wise? "Why are you going out with that one, is your head cut?"

Keepin' Dick: Meaning lookout: "Keep-dick for me while I rob this house."

Lamped: Punched: "I lamped yer man good and hard."

Lump: Lazy: "Get out of bed you big lump and get a job."

Lifted: Meaning arrested: "Wee Jimmy was lifted by the polis last night."

Mammy: Mother: ''I'm telling my Mammy on you.''

Ma: Short for Mother or Mammy: "I'll tell my Ma when I go home.''

Mon ahead: A command meaning ''Next please or come with me.''

Mucker: Mate, pal: "Alright mucker, fancy a pint?"

Oul: Meaning old or ancient: "Yer Da is wild oul."

Oul-Doll: Old Lady: "That oul-doll looks like your Ma."

Oul-Lad: Old Man: "That oul-lad lives up our street."

Pet: A term of affection for human: ''C'mon wee pet you'll have another cup of tae.''

Pinks: Potatoes: Kerrs Pinks meaning locally grown potatoes ''Jesus they are some spuds.''

Pish: Urine as in: ''I'm dying for a pish.''

Polis: Police: "The polis gave him a good hiding."

Pull: To go on a romantic conquest, usually on a Friday or Saturday night to the local dance: "Right Ma, iron my shirt will you, I'm going on the pull this evening."

Quare: Odd or peculiar: ''He is some quare boy that husband of yours.''

Queens: More potatoes as in ''Jesus those Queens are some spuds.''

Right: Assertive, usually applied at the start of a sentence: "Right, I'm away home for my tea."

Runner: Run away, flee with speed: "Here come the polis, we'll have to do a runner!"

Scundered: Embarrassed: "Look at yer man's trousers, I'm scundered for 'em!"

Sheugh: A ditch full of dirty water: ''Yer man there is as full as a sheugh.''

Shite: Excreta or rubbish: '' Where is the toilet, I need a big Shiite?''

Slabber: Drunken chat: ''You are one slabber when you are drunk.''

Snig: Remains or butt of a cigarette: ''Have you a match for my snig Mister?''

Sound: Someone or thing is easy going: "Yer Da is sound."

Spake: Pronunciation: - Speak. "Shut up and let me spake."

Spuds: Potatoes: "Get the spuds on love, I'm starving.'"

Tae: Formal pronunciation - Tea: "Put the kettle on and we'll have a wee cup of tae."

Tea: Dinner instead of supper: "Jimmy, your tea is ready."

Thon: A feckless person: ''Thon one needs a good hiding.''

Thran or Thrawn: Meaning awkward or difficult. ''Jesus but that man of yours is one thran bastard.''

Till: To or until: "Wait till yer Ma catches you?"

Trollop: Loose woman: ''She's wan trollop wearing next to nothing at Mass this morning.''

Wan: Meaning one: ''He is wan bad bastard.''

Wean: Meaning youngster: ''That is a lovely wean you have there, Mrs.''

Wee: Small: "Have a wee bun with your tea.'' "Would you like a wee bag for your shopping?"

Wild: Awful: 'That's wild weather we're having.''

Windee: Window. "Close that windee before we're foundered.''

Yarn: Talk: "I had a good yarn with the priest the other day."

Yer: Meaning 'You're': "Yer my best mate."

Yer arse in parsley: Meaning ''Don't be silly'' or ''Are you are being serious?''

Youse: You Lot. "Youse keep the noise down, I'm trying to get some effing sleep. I'm meeting the DLA man in the morning!"